Warne Gerrard Guides for Walkers

LOTHIAN AND THE SOUTH EAST BORDERS
WALKS FOR MOTORISTS

Raymond Lamont-Brown

32 sketch maps by F. Rodney Fraser
8 photographs

FREDERICK WARNE

Published by
Frederick Warne (Publishers) Ltd
40 Bedford Square
London WC1B 3HE

For Ruth who appreciates
the pleasures of walking

The photograph on the front cover is of Eildon Hills and was
taken by the author. The back cover photograph of Loch of the
Lowes and the photograph of St Abbs harbour are reproduced
by courtesy of the Scottish Tourist Board. The photographs of
Floors Castle, St Mary's Loch, the seashore at Gullane and the
church at Peebles are reproduced by courtesy of the British
Tourist Board. The photograph of the Iron Age broch at
Edin's Hall is reproduced by courtesy of the Scottish Development Department.

Publishers' Note

While every care has been taken in the compilation of
this book, the publishers cannot accept responsibility for any
inaccuracies. Things may have changed since the book was
published: paths are sometimes diverted, a concrete bridge
may replace a wooden one, stiles disappear. Please let the
publishers know if you discover anything like this on your way.

The length of each walk in this book is given in miles and
kilometres, but within the text Imperial measurements are
quoted. It is useful to bear the following approximations in
mind: 5 miles = 8 kilometres, $\frac{1}{2}$ mile = 805 metres, 1 metre
= 39.4 inches.

ISBN 0 7232 2159 6

Phototypeset by Tradespools Ltd., Frome, Somerset
Printed by Galava Printing Co. Ltd., Nelson, Lancashire
1561.381

LOTHIAN AND THE SOUTH EAST BORDERS
WALKS FOR MOTORISTS

Warne Gerrard Guides for Walkers

Walks for Motorists Series
CHESHIRE WALKS
CHILTERNS WALKS
                Northern
                Southern
COUNTY OF AVON WALKS
COUNTY OF DURHAM WALKS
DARTMOOR WALKS
DERBYSHIRE WALKS
                Northern
COTSWOLD WALKS
                Northern
                Southern
DORSET WALKS
EXMOOR WALKS
FURTHER CHESHIRE WALKS
JERSEY WALKS
LAKE DISTRICT WALKS
                Central
                Northern
                Western
LONDON COUNTRYSIDE WALKS
                North West
                North East
                South West
                South East
GREEN LONDON WALKS
                (both circular and cross country)
LOTHIAN AND SOUTH EAST BORDERS WALKS
MIDLAND WALKS
NORTHUMBERLAND WALKS
NORTH YORK MOORS WALKS
                North and East
                West and South
PEAK DISTRICT WALKS
PENDLESIDE AND BRONTË COUNTRY WALKS
SEVERN VALLEY WALKS
SNOWDONIA WALKS
                Northern
SOUTH DEVON WALKS
SOUTH DOWNS WALKS
WYE VALLEY WALKS
YORKSHIRE DALES WALKS
FURTHER DALES WALKS
Long Distance and Cross Country Walks
WALKING THE PENNINE WAY
RAMBLES IN THE DALES

Contents

			Page
	Introduction		7
Walk	1	Abbey St Bathans	12
	2	Eyemouth	15
	3	Coldingham/St Abbs	17
	4	Duns Law	20
	5	Lauder	24
	6	Gullane	27
	7	Stenton	30
	8	Tyninghame	33
	9	Spott	36
	10	Eildon Hill	39
	11	Newtown St Boswells	42
	12	Kelso	45
	13	Craik Forest	48
	14	Town Yetholm	51
	15	Abbotsford	53
	16	Huntly Covert	56
	17	St Mary's Loch	58
	18	White Meldon Settlements	61
	19	Drover's Road	64
	20	Glentress Forest	68
	21	Peebles	71
	22	Water of Leith	74
	23	Almondell	77
	24	The Monk's Road	80
	25	East Cairn Hill	82
	26	Capelaw and Clubbiedean	85
	27	Beecraigs	88
	28	Nether Hindhope	91
	29	Heatherhope	94
	30	Roman Dere Street	97

LOTHIAN AND THE SOUTH EAST BORDERS

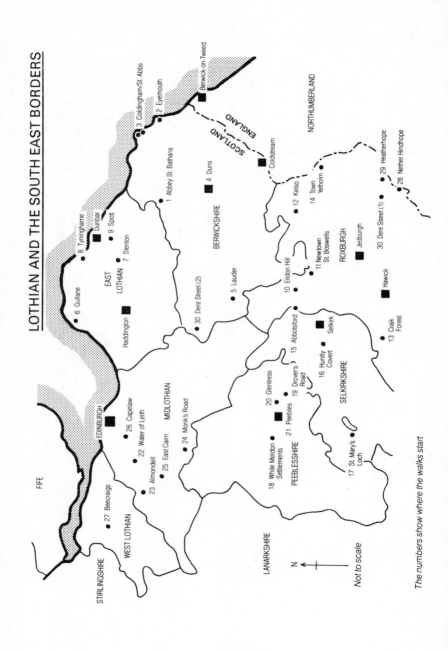

The numbers show where the walks start

Not to scale

BERWICKSHIRE

EAST LOTHIAN

MIDLOTHIAN

WEST LOTHIAN

STIRLINGSHIRE

FIFE

EDINBURGH

SELKIRKSHIRE

PEEBLESSHIRE

LANARKSHIRE

ROXBURGH

NORTHUMBERLAND

SCOTLAND
ENGLAND

1 Abbey St. Bathans
2 Eyemouth
3 Coldingham/St. Abbs
4 Duns
5 Lauder
6 Gullane
7 Stenton
8 Tyninghame
9 Spott
10 Eildon Hill
11 Newtown St. Boswells
12 Kelso
13 Craik Forest
14 Town Yetholm
15 Abbotsford
16 Huntly Covert
17 St. Mary's Loch
18 White Meldon Settlements
19 Drover's Road
20 Glentress
21 Peebles
22 Water of Leith
23 Almondell
24 Monk's Road
25 East Cairn
26 Capelaw
27 Beecraigs
28 Nether Hindhope
29 Heatherhope
30 Dere Street (1)
30 Dere Street (2)

Berwick-on-Tweed
Coldstream
Haddington
Dunbar
Selkirk
Jedburgh
Hawick

Introduction

Walkers in the south-east borderland of Scotland are in for a treat. For here in this romantic land, where Scotland's destiny was forged, are lands which have come lately on the tourist scene and are basically 'unspoiled' in the way perhaps best appreciated by those who walked the area between the wars. The scope of this book is for the motorist who wishes to park his car safely and conveniently, and take to paths and roads on foot.

According to modern local government the area covered is Lothian and the Borders, which takes in the more familiar counties of West Lothian, Midlothian, East Lothian, Peeblesshire, Selkirkshire, Roxburghshire and Berwickshire. To the south-east of Edinburgh rises a portion of the southern uplands bisected by the highroads to England. Beyond the Lammermuir and the Moorfoot Hills, green slopes unfold to the border, criss-crossed by the valleys and moors of the river Tweed and its tributaries. Their charming, unfolding outlines are mantled with heather and lush grass, broken only by the volcanic cones of the Eildon Hills which sprout defiantly from the Tweed valley.

Starting at Edinburgh, the finest view of the south-east uplands is from the 833ft summit of Arthur's Seat—that twin-peaked mountain of volcanic rock in the heart of Scotland's capital. Reaching the summit easily by well-trodden paths, the walker can take in Holyrood Park below, the view of the mighty bridges of Forth and its coast to the west, and south-east to the glorious Border Country.

The Moorfoot Hills and the dry, heather-locked slopes of Lammermuir throw out taunting challenges to the seeker of solitude. Access to the Lammermuirs is easily gained from the highflung B6355 out of Tranent, via Pencaitland, Gifford and Preston, or by its parallel branch to Duns, via Longformacus. Off the dead-end track from Longformacus to the reservoir of the Watch Water, and south to Westruther village, lies the Dye Water. To enjoy these hills walkers can park safely at both Longformacus and the reservoir. Flanking the Lammermuirs are the fine stretches of coastal scenery accessible to walkers from St Abbs, Barns Ness and Tyninghame.

For the Moorfoots go south out of Edinburgh to Penicuik on the A702 and thence via the A702 to its junction with the A703 for Peebles. Here is the peaceful forest of Glentress, now laid out by the Forestry Commission with spacious walks among the plantations of tall Norwegian and Sitka spruce and Douglas fir. From these plantations can be seen impressive views across the Tweed valley to the south.

From Peebles and Innerleithen, 7 miles away, there are a number of fine walks. Take the road from Traquair, south of Innerleithen, at the junction of the B7062 and the B709, and enjoy the 6 miles over Minch Moor. Several old tracks run north by Minch Moor Hill (1859ft) through the forest land to the east. Descend then to the A708 and the Yarrow Ford on the river Tweed, casting an eye to Wallace's Trench. This mysterious shallow ditch was named after the Scottish patriot and chieftain Sir William Wallace (*circa* 1270–1305), who led the Scottish armies against Edward I. Wallace plagued Edward with guerrilla warfare in Ettrick Forest, which was once wider in scope than now. The ditch is probably an earlier boundary line.

The walker of the south-east borderland has the chance too of identifying and following the ancient Border roads. The Wheel Causeway, south-east of Hawick, is one of the ancient roads that cross the border from Scotland to England. Take the A6088 south from Bonchester Bridge, then the B6357, turning after ½ mile. Seek out the safe parking where the road becomes rough, and follow the old track uphill which winds southwards. See how the old tracks traversed the high, exposed, rugged country, and note how early man used the terrain. The hills of Bonchester, Rubers Law and Eildon are spotted with prehistoric hill-forts and camps, all welcoming landmarks to the walker of the upland highways.

For those who wish to pace the hills in the footsteps of the Roman legionaries, there is the impressive Dere Street, ribboning over the Cheviot hills, and following the Pennine Way for part of its length. Exciting explorations can be made if you follow the minor road which leaves the A68 3 miles north of Carter Bar, running eastwards across the Cheviots. At Pennymuir, 5 miles along this minor road, the way crosses Dere Street. Park here safely and follow a wall northwards alongside the partly overgrown Roman road which is marked with yellow ringed posts; here, too, one can see the remains of the quarries which provided the stone for the roads. South of Pennymuir, the modern road follows the line of Dere Street for around 1 mile, crossing Kale Water at Tow Ford, which was paved by the Romans. Dere Street continues as the path across the gentle northern slopes of Woden Law (1388ft). Here the Roman surveyors placed the road to gain a ridge leading up to the main Cheviot chain and to England. Pause at the summit of Woden Law and people, in the mind's eye, the prehistoric hill-fort and the Roman siege-works. From here is a panoramic view of Dere Street as it runs north-west to the Roman fort of *Trimontium*, at Newstead, nestling below the Eildon Hills.

From the south one can enter the Borders through the A6105/A1 link at Berwick-on-Tweed via the A697 at Coldstream, the A68 at Carter Bar, or the minor road, off the B6320 Chollerford to Otterburn road, at Kielder (to Bonchester Bridge).

Footpaths and other interesting walkways of the Lothian/Borders

Hopetoun House—home of the Marquis of Linlithgow. Stately

Home. Nature Trail. Off the B924. Open every afternoon, except Thursday and Friday, from the end of April to the end of September. Two miles, woodland and shore. Details: Hopetoun Estate Office, South Queensferry, West Lothian EH30 9LS.

Almondell and Calder Wood—country park. Take A8 at Broxburn. River and woodland. Details: Park Ranger, 81 Mansfield, East Calder.

Innerwick—general walkway. Contact, East Lothian Country Council, Dunbar Education Area Sub-Committee, District Office, Dunbar.

The National Trust in the Lothians and South-east Borders

The House of the Binns—historic home of the Dalyell family. Visitor trail. Open Easter and 1 May to 30 September daily except Friday, 2.00–5.30.

The Georgian House, 7 Charlotte Square, Edinburgh—a typical Scottish Georgian residence. Audio-visual show. Open 24 March to 22 October. Mondays–Saturdays 10.00–5.00, Sundays 2.00–5.00. 28 October to 31 January, Saturday and Sunday only.

Gladstone's Land, Edinburgh—six-storey tenement of 1620, in Royal Mile. Times of opening various.

Preston Mill, East Lothian—working, water mill. Open 1 April–30 September, Monday–Saturday 10.00–12.30 and 2.00–7.30, Sunday 2.00–7.30; 1 October to 31 March, closes 4.30.

Priorwood Gardens, Melrose—open 24 March to mid October, Monday to Saturday 10.00–6.00, Sunday 1.30–5.30; mid-October to 24 December, Monday 2.00–5.30, Tuesday to Saturday 10.00–5.30.

Suntrap, Gogerbank, Lothian—garden trail. Monday-Friday 9.00–5.00 and (1 March to 31 October only) Saturday and Sunday 2.30–5.00.

Tourist Board addresses

Directors of the Border tourist boards are anxious to receive suggestions for the improvement of walking tourism in their areas. Please send them notice of any rights of way which have become obstructed, or pathways which have become dangerous. The main tourist board headquarters are:

East Lothian District Council, Tourist Office, Dunbar, East Lothian.

The Scottish Tourist Board, 23 Ravelston Terrace, Edinburgh EH4 3EU.

The Director of Tourism, Tourist Information Centre, Town Hall, Market Place, Selkirk, Selkirkshire.

The Director of Tourism, Tourist Information Centre, Common Haugh, Hawick, Roxburghshire.

The Director of Tourism, Tourist Information Centre, Town Hall, High Street, Peebles, Peeblesshire.

West Lothian District Council, Tourist Office, Linlithgow, West Lothian.

Berwickshire Tourist Office, Duns, Berwickshire.

Information centres are also to be found at: Henderson Park Coldstream; Home Arms Car Park, Eyemouth; Town Hall, Galashiels; Murray's Green, Jedburgh; Turret House, Kelso; Priorswood, Nr the Abbey, Melrose. Lothian information centres are to be found at Dunbar, Linlithgow, Middleton, North Berwick, Pathhead and Pencraig (follow road signs). For a brochure of STB information centres ask for (free) publication 2908/03/40M.

Border and Lothian Festivals

The Folklore Year includes the following events:

January 25—Burns night. The occasion to celebrate the birth of the Scottish poet Robert Burns.

February—around the second of the month is the 'Jeddart Ba' Game'. A curious folklore ball game at Jedburgh.

June—usually the third week. Beltane bonfire festival at Peebles.

June—third week. Festival at Melrose.

June—Saturday, depending on tides. Children's Gala Day at Cockenzie.

July—third week, Friday and Saturday evenings. 'Cleiking the Devil' at Innerleithen.

August—second week. 'The Burry Man' and Ferry Fair at South Queensferry.

Scotland's Country Code

Over the years a ten-point Country Code has been evolved in Scotland, taking into consideration the special needs of the countryside.

Perhaps the worst danger to the Scottish countryside is fire. So extinguish all campfires thoroughly, and do not carelessly throw away cigarettes or lighted matches. Bottles and jars left around can also catch the sun's rays and cause fire. Make a mental note of where fire-fighting equipment is stored (water buckets, sand and twig-brushes are placed in many country areas alongside a Fire Warning notice).

Fasten all gates, keep dogs under proper control and keep to the established paths over farmland. In the Borders you may come across a gate with the words *Stik the yett*. This is old Border dialect for 'Shut the gate'.

Leaving no litter about is common sense, as is avoiding damaging fences, hedges, walls and flora. Today it is more important than ever to protect wild life and water supplies.

By and large the law governing rights of way is the same in Scotland as for the rest of Britain, except that the attitude towards trespassers is more lenient in Scotland. Providing that no damage is done, or interference made to property, landowners in Scotland are a reasonable bunch. Remember, however, that in Scotland bulls are allowed into fields with public footpaths.

When using maps, other than the ones provided in the text here, check that they are up to date, for in Scotland a footpath can be closed if it has been disused for 20 years.

The walks described in this book are set out on official rights of way, or on permitted footpaths, or on public access areas. One or two paths (noted) are by kind permission of the owners. With such rights, of course, go the responsibilities guided by the Country Code.

Supplementary maps, compasses, whistles, torches, loose change are all paraphernalia for the walker. Cameras, sketch pads, flora and fauna indentification books and binoculars are to be taken at the walker's discretion. Strong, waterproof shoes with thick soles are essential, as is comfortable, lightweight, waterproof clothing to suit the season. A walking stick can be useful for steep places, and a small back pack for food (if a car picnic is not contemplated) and a first aid kit.

Throughout the book, where there are points of special interest to the walker, a short passage giving information that might be of interest has been added at the end of the relevant walks. These are included under the heading **Special Interest**.

Walk 1   Abbey St Bathans

5 miles (8 km)

OS sheet 67

This river valley and gentle hill walk is best reached by taking the
A6112 Grantshouse road out of Duns; turn left along first the B6365
and then the A6355, following the signs to Abbey St Bathans. Alternatively, take the turning for the village, marked just south of
Cockburnspath on the A1.

Legend has it that a Christian settlement, once called St Bathan's
Chapel, was built in what is now known as Abbey St Bathans, in the
seventh century by a visiting missionary, Bothan, Prior of Old
Melrose. Although the remains of an ancient chapel were found here
in the nineteenth century, its exact origin is uncertain. It is certain,
however, that at the end of the twelfth century a priory of 12
Cistercian nuns was founded here by Ada, Countess of Dunbar, and
daughter of King William the Lion. Although the priory was
extensively damaged in a raid by the English (11 August 1544), the
east gable and north wall remain and are incorporated into the
present parish church.

The walk begins at the parish church situated off the main road to the
right in the centre of the village, where safe, if limited, parking is to be
had.

While at the church look within the recess in the east wall for the
worn stone figure of a former prioress with the little dog at her feet; she
was a contemporary of Geoffrey Chaucer, who wrote of such a
prioress and her small dogs. Not far from the churchyard, in the
grounds of St Bathans House, is the Holy Well, visited for its curative
properties. A nearby path still bears the name of Pilgrim Path.

The name of the village is also surrounded with mystery, since
neither Bothan's chapel nor Ada's priory ever achieved abbey status.
The prefix 'Abbey' probably derives from local confusion about the
precise nature of the church.

From the church, walk to the main road, turn left and head out of
the village to a ford and footbridge on the left crossing the River
Whiteadder. At this point the Whiteadder has become a fully fledged
river after its birth in the East Lothian hills. On the far side of the river
turn right at the signpost and climb up through the wood. Pass
through the gate into a field near the mill and descend to the rough
track below. Then by crossing the stile, turn left up the track walking

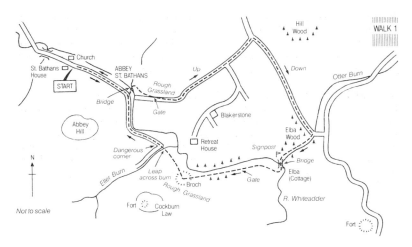

for around 1 mile onto the main road. At the road turn right down the hill to the entrance of Elba Wood. Do not cross Otter Burn where the road bends to the left, but turn right into the wood, keeping the burn on your left. Keep Blackerstone Farm on your right throughout the walk.

Walk down the forest track to the first signpost, taking the left fork. Follow the track over the river, crossing it at the footbridge. This valley contains almost a third of the oak-dominated woodland in the Borders, and sports the evergreen and pedunculate varieties whilst another goodly proportion of the trees are Douglas fir.

Look out, too, for the huge banks of rhododendrons. The valley, flanked on one side of its eastern end by the semi bogland of Drakemire Strips, is an important site for woodland flowers like dog's mercury and rosebay willowherb as well as various species of birds and insects. The river is mainly the home of the brown trout and permits to fish are obtainable from the local angling association in the village.

From the footbridge turn right past the cottage, and follow the signposts along the edge of the field to a stile on the ridge above the field. Have more than a first glance at the cottage marked on maps as 'Elba'. Scholars aver that the name may be derived from the Gaelic word *eil*, meaning a hill, and *both*, a dwelling. Locals support the equally plausible explanation that the name refers to the sharp bend in the river at this point making an elbow (or, 'elba', in Border dialect). Look near the cottage for the remains of the copper mine which was worked in the 1700s. The mine was re-opened in 1825 but soon ran out of economically workable copper.

Having crossed the stile, walk beside the wood on the right to another stile, and beyond it to the gate leading onto the hill and Edin's Hall Broch. Descend from the broch, through the field opposite

13

Retreat House on the other side of the river. The valley side is steep and shelves to the Eller Burn which is leapable. Cross the burn and climb the steep bank to the famous 'Toot Corner' (this is where motorists are requested to toot their horns!). At the road turn right and walk into the village and back to the church.

Special Interest: Edin's Hall Broch
In simple terms a broch is a prehistoric stone tower. This broch is only one of ten Iron Age brochs known in Lowland Scotland. It measures some 80ft in diameter and the walls vary in thickness from 10–20ft. The walls contain a series of cells and chambers. An additional defensive system of earthworks and ditches can still be seen round the broch, which now only stands to around 5ft.

Walk 2

Eyemouth

5 miles (8 km)

OS sheet 67

The basis of this walk is the old smugglers' route along the cliffs from Eyemouth to Linkim Shore and thence via Fleurs valley, where contraband was stashed and buried, to the A1107, between Coldingham and Eyemouth down which the 'gaugers' (the dialect word for excise officer) used to gallop. The walk is not arduous and is straightforward.

Eyemouth is the largest centre of population in modern Berwickshire. The town, which has long been recognized as one of the most important fishing ports on the east coast of Scotland, can be reached from the A1 by taking the B6355 from Ayton, or watching for turn-off signs just south of Cockburnspath (route from the north) or just north of Berwick-on-Tweed (route from the south). Eyemouth has been a Burgh of Barony since 1597.

Park in Eyemouth on the quayside; or High Street car park near the sea front (parking here is free). Get the atmosphere of the place by first wandering around the network of narrow streets which dissect the old part of the town. The higgledy-piggledy architecture was designed, locals say, to make it easier for the smugglers to dodge the excise men. Relics of the eighteenth- and nineteenth-century smugglers' age are everywhere in the town. Cross the footbridge by the quay and follow the path round to Gunsgreen House—near the house is the entrance to an old smugglers' secret passage. Cromwell visited Eyemouth in 1650, and the nearby tower to Gunsgreen (used as Eyemouth Golf Clubhouse) is associated with him. Gunsgreenhill gives a fine view of this busy fishing port on the Eye Water and the green mounds around give the place a scenic character.

Begin the walk proper back over the bridge at the High Street car park. From here make for the bay, skirting the caravan park, and climb towards the edge of the headland via steps cut into the bank. On the headland is the coastguard station near to the remains of a sixteenth-century fortress which was garrisoned by French troops.

Down towards the shore is Hairy Ness and the tide-covered rocks of Buss Craig. Spare a thought, as you watch the relentless sea, for the old Eyemouth tale of 'Black Friday'. For on Friday 14 October 1881, 129 fishermen of Eyemouth—almost half of the whole adult male population of the town—were lost when the fishing fleet hit bad weather.

15

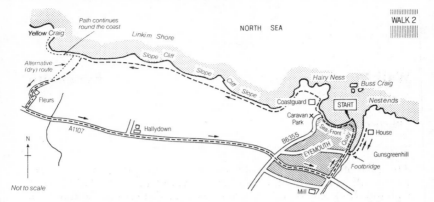

Relatives of the missing stood for hours on the headland watching for the fleet to return.

Follow the path round the edge of the caravan site along the cliff tops. When you come to the end of the tarred path, take the sign-posted footpath to the right, heading away from the town. This path is uncomplicated and direct and takes you through the fields, crossing three stiles before you reach the gully above Linkim Shore. Leave the path where it meets the stream and head up the gully.

With its many bays and prominent headlands, the coast of Berwickshire has long been a classic hunting ground for geologists; one of the best sample areas in the world. On this walk are extensive deposits of exposed volcanic material. A wide range of seabirds can also be observed, gannets, fulmars, terns and a multitude of gulls. It is fascinating to stand along the cliff for a while and watch the seagulls on the wing. Watch them ride the air almost stationary with a slight swaying of their outstretched wings as they rise and fall through the thermal currents by the cliff edge. With webbed feet held tightly under the tail, like the retracted undercarriage of an aeroplane, they drop into the water to seize floating food from trawlers. Lowering their legs as they descend, they settle on the water and spend hours snatching at morsels.

Along the cliff-top path are many coastal plants including brookweed on the damper cliffs, fennel, wild cabbage, thrift and fine local strains of sea pinks, sea bindweed and viper's bugloss. On the rocky shores sea-campions and sea-milkwort flourish.

Follow the stream up the wooded gully until you come to the fork in the waters. Take the right-hand fork as your guide and walk for about $\frac{1}{4}$ mile until you join the farm track of Fleurs. This track will bring you out onto the A1107. (If the gully is too muddy, walk along the cliff top until you reach a path going left, turn onto this and follow it until you reach the farm track.)

Once on the A1107 walk to Eyemouth via Hallydown Farm. Cross the B6355 and follow the road down to Eyemouth bridge over the Eye Water. Down to your right are the remains of the old railway station, and shipbuilding yard. Follow this road back to the car park.

16

Walk 3
6 miles (9.5 km)

Coldingham/St Abbs

This walk may be remembered for its colour, for the landscape changes colour and captures the imagination. The heath and rock and cropped grass, purple in the sun, blue-grey in the mist, deep dark brown in a November rain-storm, is a fitting match for the dramatic blues and greys of the North Sea.

Although granted status as a burgh in 1638, because of its size and importance, Coldingham is now a small village which becomes very busy in the summer with visitors to the coast. Called *Urbs Coludi* by the monastic chronicler, the Venerable Bede, Coldingham is reached by the A1107, either the A1 at Burnmouth (south) via Eyemouth or the A1 at Cockburnspath (north).

Start the walk at the priory gate facing the old market cross. (Free parking—park sensibly please!) Turn right and walk to the junction of the A1107 and the B6438 a few yards away. Follow this road for just over a mile until you come to the made-up road to Northfield, and walk past the houses until you get to the place where the road crosses a burn. Simply follow the surfaced road without turning left or right as this leads up to the lighthouse. All around there are signs of prehistoric settlements, usually on the brows of the hills. Earthworks and ditches can still be seen, dating back to the Iron Age (*circa* 500 BC). On your left is Coldingham Loch and nearby Westloch House, and on your right is a long narrow loch with an outlet into Horsecastle Bay. As you approach the sea above Pettico Wick, the northern sea-coast stretch of Coldingham Moor opens up. Look away into the distance for the ruins of Fast Castle. It has long been popularly accepted as the original 'Wolf's Crag' mentioned in Sir Walter Scott's *Bride of Lammermuir*. The gloomy castle was a fortress of the Home family, who ruled much of the district.

Trees are sparse here but look for the whin, the sea heath and the heathers, cross-leaved and bell varieties. As you approach St Abb's Head, cormorants, gannets, gulls, fulmars and guillemots can be seen.

The path sweeps round in a wide U-shape and leads away to the lighthouse at St Abb's Head (310ft). Walk past the lighthouse buildings and make directly for the loch where the path skirts the south end

Lighthouse

St. Abb's Head

Pettico Wick

End of unfenced road

Cliffs

Coldingham Loch

Forts

Wuddy Rocks

Bell Hill

Slope

N

NORTH SEA

(Old Path)

Not to scale

B6438

St Abbs

Coldingham Bay

START

Haven

△

The Mount

† Priory

COLDINGHAM

of the loch. Turn left where the path forks, making for Bell Hill above the strangely named Wuddy Rocks. At Bell Hill the path comes near to the cliff edge, but is safe and well-defined. Follow this path for about ½ mile where it joins the B6438. Turn left and walk down into St Abbs.

This quaint fishing village, popular with photographers and aquasport devotees, takes its name from St Ebba, a sister of King Oswy of Northumbria, who landed on the coast at this point in 640. She presided over an ecclesiastical community in this area, as did her sisters St Helen and St Bey in nearby locations. It's worth spending a little time exploring the steep, irregular, narrow streets which run down to the harbour—note the architecture of the fishermen's houses and the so-called 'dolls' houses' where they kept their gear. Both the harbour and the church were built by a member of the brewing family of Usher.

Leave St Abbs by the coastal path south of the village and walk along the cliffs by Coldingham Bay. Note the many 'huts' by the shore—once it was an important stroke of snobbish 'one-upmanship' to have a hut here. The path winds round to St Abb's Haven. At St Veda's path (a restaurant, where the path goes down to the beach) head for the Mount and follow the road down to the wooded valley and Milldown. This road leads round to a more major road into the village, then to the B6438 and back to the priory gates.

Special Interest: Coldingham Priory

A church was founded here in 1098 by King Edgar, which with the surrounding land grew into the famous priory, dedicated to St Mary and St Cuthbert and run by Benedictine monks from Durham Cathedral. The priory was much damaged by the Earl of Hertford in 1545, and by Cromwell in 1648. The ruins have been extensively renovated and now house one of the oldest parish churches in Scotland where public worship is still observed. Watch for the ghost of the nun who was walled up here as a punishment; her story is told by Sir Walter Scott in *Marmion*. Look, too, on the outside, for the Romanesque arcade and string courses surmounted by lancet windows at the east end, and, within the church, at the Early English (1189–1280) arcade with foliated columns that forms a gallery round the north and east walls. Fragments of the south transept and ruins of the monastic refectory remain. For some years now there have been a series of excavations at the priory during the summer.

Important note: The new owner of St Abb's Head (190 acres) is the National Trust for Scotland, who are managing the area jointly with the Scottish Wildlife Trust. The NTS welcomes thoughtful walkers and would appreciate reports of any vandalism encountered.

Walk 4   Duns Law

8 miles (13 km)

OS sheet 67

Pick a clear day with bright weather to get the most out of this walk.
Take a full day to do the round. Stout shoes and a picnic would be the
basic extras for the walk, as a large part of it is through woodland.

Duns takes its name from the Celtic word *dun*, meaning a hill
defence, and one of the highlights of this walk is an exploration of the
ancient settlement located on the hill known as Duns Law. The town
emerged in importance from 1489 when King James VI made it a
burgh. Because it is close to the Border, the town was raided many
times by the English and in 1558 was completely devastated. It was
rebuilt and developed into a popular watering spa in the eighteenth
century when mineral springs were discovered here in 1747. Duns was
the county town of Berwickshire from 1903 to 1975.

Park in the officially sited car park (free) in Market Square. Head out
of Market Square into Castle Street. Off this street is Newtown Street,
which houses the town's administrative office and the 'Jim Clark
Room', the permanent memorial to the world motor racing champion
who was killed in Germany in 1968.

Walk up Castle Street and continue past Tiendhill Road, on the
right, and you will come to Duns Castle entrance. From the Pavilion
Lodge at the top of the main driveway you can obtain a glimpse of the
castle which is strictly private property. The imposing building has
been the seat of the Hay family since 1698, but the history of the building goes back to 1320, when the original building was set up by
Randolph, Earl of Murray, nephew of King Robert the Bruce. The
present castle is the work of James Gillespie Graham.

Immediately opposite the Pavilion Lodge is the cairn marking the
birthplace of Duns's most famous native, John Duns Scotus (*c.*
1265–1308), whose philosophy and teaching continue to command
world respect. From here can be seen something of the expanse of the
castle estate to the right, which is well worth a special visit as it covers
an area of woodland containing many species of bird, animal and
plantlife, as well as a fine stretch of water known as the Hen Poo',
which is the haunt of wild fowl and sanctuary of many types of birds.
As the wildlife here is strictly protected, a permit is necessary for a
visit and such may be obtained from the Reserve Warden, Mr W.
Waddel, of The Mount, Duns.

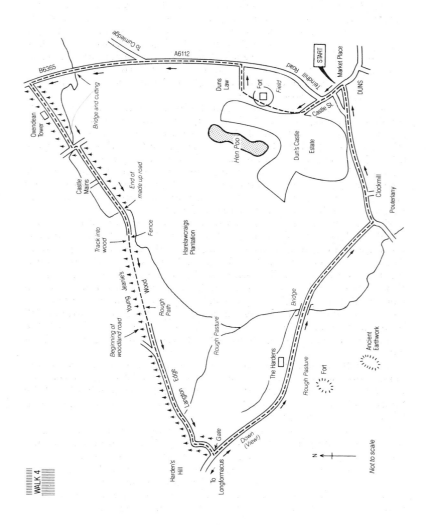

WALK 4

To Cumledge
A6112
B6365
Oxendean Tower
Bridge and cutting
Castle Mains
End of made up road
Track into wood
Fence
Harelawcraigs Plantation
Jeanie's Wood
Young Wood
Rough Path
Beginning of woodland road
Langton Edge
Rough Pasture
Harden's Hill
To Longformacus
Gate
Down (View!)
The Hardens
Rough Pasture
Bridge
Fort
Ancient Earthwork
Hen Poo
Dun's Castle Estate
Duns Law
Fort
Field
Castle St.
Teindhill Road
START
Market Place
DUNS
Clockmill
Pouterlany
N
Not to scale

21

Not far from the Lodge is a sign-posted track leading to the summit of Duns Law. The path is a well-defined woodland track leading to one of the most impressive views in the Borders. Some 715ft above sea-level, it is an invigorating spot, for from here stretches away the ancient land of the Merse. The Merse was the old political term used to designate all the country between the Lammermuirs and the Cheviots. This land was held for the king of Scotland by the Earl of March (a secondary title still held by the Earl of Wemyss). Look to the east where lies the Berwick coast, Northumberland and Holy Island; to the north are the Lammermuirs and Cockburn Law; and to the south, the Cheviot Hills and England. Look, too, on the hill, for the Covenanter's Stone.

Descend the hill from the fort and join the path to the main road, turning left along the A6112. On your right will be signs for the farm-stead of Ashfield and Johnsfield. Walk for about ¾ mile and take the left-hand fork (B6365). Look for the turning for Oxendean Tower; the first turning you come to on the left is to an old quarry. (N.B. This part of the walk—until you arrive at the next section of main road—is farm property and protected forest land. Visitors are welcome, so do your part to keep it so. Children should be supervised and dogs leashed. Watch out for newly planted trees.)

Follow the road up to Oxendean Tower, once an old family fortified dwelling. Past the tower the road turns to the right past buildings (note the wind pump away to your left) and comes to a T-junction. Take the first left and first right and make for Castle Mains. Follow this track for about ½ mile until its width peters out in Young Jeanie's Wood. For ½ mile you have to make your way through protected woodland, so respect the privilege of being there. Soon you will join up with a woodland track along Langton Edge; keep the Hardens Hill broadcasting masts on your right. As you meet up again with the tarmac road, Raecleugh Head is front right and Langtonlees front left.

Turn left at the main road and pass The Hardens and Duns Golf Course on your left, you will join the A6105 for Duns at Pouterlany, where you turn left. Through Clockmill, Duns High School and the South Lodge of Duns Castle will be on your left; follow this main road back to the market place.

While on this walk keep a look out especially for the primroses in season, the bluebells and crow-wheat. Both of the common ferns, lady and male, proliferate. All along the Borders keep away from the hogweed as this can cause weals and irritation; try to distinguish the latter from cow parsley. All common strains of birds are to be found along this walk, but look particularly for the magpie, the yellow-hammer, the blue tit, the greenfinch and the song thrush.

Special Interest: Covenanter's Stone

This block of red sandstone which was enclosed in 1878 to protect it from souvenir hunters, was the one on which the Covenanter's were said to have planted their great banner. 'Covenanters' was the name given to the signatories of the Scottish National Covenant in 1638, who were pledged to uphold the Presbyterian faith against prelacy and popery. Here on Duns Law in 1639 some 2,000 Covenanters, under the command of General Alexander Leslie, prepared to do battle with the army of Charles I, who wished to force Episcopalianism on the Scots. No battle took place, a pacification was arranged and the Scottish army was disbanded.

Important note: The Forestry Commission from time to time re-aligns footpaths to take into consideration wildlife needs and tree conservation. New fencing and blocked paths may be put up *without prior notice* as a result of vandalism or commercial policy. The Forestry Commission walk at Pease Bay (formerly Duns and now part of Lammermuir Forest) is not to be maintained. The attractive walks a Cardona ($3\frac{1}{2}$ miles east of Peebles) are extant.

Walk 5   Lauder

4 miles (6·5 km)

OS sheet 73

For walkers wishing to assess a 'typical' Border town in a 'typical' Border setting then this walk is the one for them. For Lauder has all the magic ingredients to make up a Border habitation. Set 600ft above sea-level, on the banks of the River Leader, Lauder is surrounded on three sides by the Lammermuir Hills. It seems that the town was given a Royal Charter during the reign of William the Lion (1165–1214), but the original documents were mislaid.

It's interesting to whet one's appetite for the area by visiting Thirlestane, the home of the Maitland family, Earls of Lauderdale. Until the sixteenth century, the castle was known as Lauder Fort, and was richly adorned with avenues, pavilions, courts and stately entrances, trees and shrubs by John, Duke of Lauderdale.

Choose stout shoes for this walk as, although the path is easy to follow, the ground tends to be rough, the grass longish and bracken abounds. Smooth soled shoes are not recommended.

Park in the municipal car park in the centre of the town, opposite the gates of Thirlestane Castle. Leave the car park from the exit opposite the castle and turn left. This takes you into The Row, a corruption of the Rue de Roi, the king's road to his hunting lodge. The road is probably the oldest part of Lauder. Follow the road round its sharp left-hand turn into West High Street. Here is a concourse of roads. Head left into Crofts Road and take the second main turning right into Manse Road. After some hundred yards the road disappears at an open area and you continue forward by a path. The path bears to the right and will take you past two plantation strips up a gradual rise. When you have passed the second plantation strip the hill slopes fold out before you as you climb up Staunchley Hill. As the path flattens out round the middle of the hill, pause and look back at the town. In the foreground is Chester Hill and the way to Galashiels, and all around are relics of the dozens of small Celtic farmsteads which once dotted the course of the Leader River.

As you pass the summit of the hill, up on the right, the path remains level and then drops down gradually towards the burn where three paths come together. One leads on to the road across Lauder Common and passes under the electricity pylons. Take the path to

24

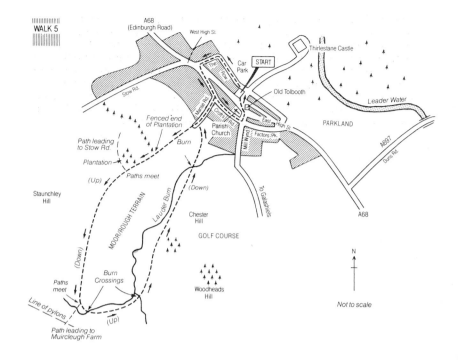

your left which follows the burn and crosses it. On the right-hand side of the burn walk on until you come to another burn. Cross this and you are on the lower slopes of Woodheads Hill.

The path now leads you forward and leaves the burn; you have crossed two tributary burns which make up the Lauder Burn on your left. There is a wood to your right up the hill and you are making for a smaller belt of trees on Chester Hill flanking the golf course. You will be gradually descending now. Keep to the path as it closes with the burn—which you cross—and it will bring you safely to a path parallel to the made-up road at Manse Road. This will bring you out again into Crofts Road. A leisurely supplementary stroll along the wide main street—Market Place to East High Street, and back to Factors Park—and its hinterland of wandering lanes and narrow alleys, gives much of the air of the old-world atmosphere of the town. Follow Crofts Road round into the Market Place, past the parish church and the Tolbooth, across from which is the car park.

Special Interest: Church and Tolbooth

The parish church was· built on the present site in 1673. It is constructed on the plan of a Greek Cross, with an unusual octagonal bell-

25

tower. Facing the church, in the centre of the town, is the Tolbooth, built in 1318. Most Scottish towns had a tolbooth which corresponded to the English town hall. Originally thatched, it has not changed greatly in appearance over the centuries. The ground floor of the building was used as a gaol until 1843. Many a person accused of witchcraft was imprisoned here, for all around are name relics of witches—Witches Knowe, Witches Pool, Ducking Pool—grim reminders of the days when those suspected of witchcraft were thrown into deep pools to ascertain their guilt or innocence.

4½ miles (7 km)

OS sheet 66

Anyone who takes this walk sees how the character of the village of Gullane, and its survival, have been dictated by coastal erosion. It was something of an important local centre of the old environs of Luffness from the twelfth century, when its church, dedicated to St Andrew, was built at the landward end of Sandy Loan. As time passed and the wind howled, sand encroached on the settlement, and by 1612 the church was so inundated with sand that an Act was passed in the Scottish Parliament to build a new church at the less vulnerable, nearby village of Dirleton. The last vicar of Gullane, legend has it, was sacked by James VI for smoking tobacco. The ruins of the church are worth a look, as are the walls of Saltcoats Castle, with its sixteenth-century dovecote. Today Gullane is a mecca for golfers. One of the features of this walk is the variety of wildlife that is to be seen throughout the year. Apart from a large number of species of bird to be seen, a very wide range of shells is to be found on Gullane beaches, particularly along the tide line. There are numerous varieties of plants too and it is interesting to pay particular attention to the seaweeds found hereabouts.

To arrive at Gullane, take the A1 from Edinburgh, via Musselburgh. At the motor inn at the roundabout at Wallyford turn left onto the A198. Keep on this road, via Longniddry and Aberlady, and you will pass straight into Gullane. If you are coming from the south, leave the A1 at Haddington, turning onto the A6137 to Aberlady and from there, right on to the A198 at Aberlady.

Begin the walk in the established car park, which is between the village and the sea. Walk back towards the village and follow the path as it bends round to a fork. Take the left-hand path along the Gullane Bents, and make for the scrub area to the left and the sea. Since 1935 this area has been in the hands of the local council, who neglected it, making the 'lagoon' of sands which front Gullane Bay. Erosion was further encouraged when this area was used as a rehearsal area for the Normandy landings of World War II. Reclamation started in 1956, when marram grass, sea buckthorn and wooden posts with brushwood fences were set out. The task of fighting the erosion continues, so keep to the paths and avoid the individual and marked plots of vegetation which are 'in growth'.

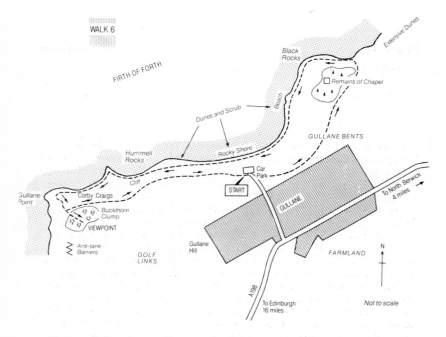

Follow the path round the scrub to the West Links, and keep left all the way to Black Rocks. Here on the right are the remains of an old chapel. Walk on until you meet the path leading up to the car park and, ignoring this, keep left across the dunes past the black diamond shaped marker. Turn left and follow the uninterrupted pathway for just over a mile. This will bring you right past Gullane Bay and Hummel Rocks to Gullane Point.

From the rocks on Gullane Point walk directly inland, turning left onto a wide grassy track, keeping to the left of a large dune. On your immediate left is Corby Crags. You will now come to a junction of several paths; go up the hill on to a rough road to the top of Buckthorn Clump, a fine viewpoint. Downhill are to be seen the lines of concrete anti-tank barriers of World War II, and the Aberlady Bay Nature Reserve (reached by going 2 miles south of Gullane on the A198)—it's walkable by continuing round the dunes. This point affords a fine view of the sandy shore of Gullane, from which, fans of Robert Louis Stevenson will remember, Alan Breck made his exciting final escape in *Catriona*.

Return to the junction and take the path to the right keeping the bracken on the left. Once at the shore take the lower path uphill to the top of the cliff. Pass the tank barriers, which lie across the path, and walk straight on along the head of the cliff, ignoring the tracks down the hill to the left. Pause for a moment and look at the long view from

28

east to west along the Firth of Forth. To the south-west, is Edinburgh marked by the twin peaks of Arthur's Seat. Left of this point stretches the long range of the Pentland Hills. See, too, out in the Firth, the lighthouse island of Inchkeith (a part of Fife Region), named after the Keith family, to whom it was granted by Royal Charter in 1010. After the Battle of Pinkie, 1547, the English planted a fort on the island, but from 1549 to 1567 it was held and garrisoned by the French. Inchkeith was visited in 1773 by Dr Johnson and James Boswell, who found 'very good grass but rather a profusion of thistles!'

Inland of this cliff top are the golf links of Gullane Golf Club, on land once partially used to train racehorses. Where the path passes fences beside (Alas!) a refuse tip, turn sharp left down the hill. Keep right to join the rough road that will bring you back to the car park.

Walk 7

Stenton

8 miles (13 km)

OS sheet 67

At the beginning of this walk is a well-maintained and fascinating forest trail, through an area sadly neglected by tourists who speed north on the A1 nearby. To reach the start of the walk, turn left at the village of East Linton and follow the signs for Stenton. When you reach the B6370, turn left into the village, and then right to Rushlaw West Mains. Just past the farm on the left are signposts to the Forest Trail of Pressmennan. The walk includes several gradients.

The walk begins at the official Lothian Region car park. Out of the car park walk straight forward through the forest trail (a booklet is available on the trail, in the car park) and make for the viewpoint. Alternatively you can turn left at the car park and follow the path skirting Pressmennan lake, which was artificially set out some 160 years ago. It's title is worth noting, challenging as it does the Lake of Menteith's (Perthshire) claim to be the only *lake* in Scotland.

Assuming that you go to the viewpoint, Lothian Edge and Dunbar Common are south, Dunbar town and the sea are east, the village of Garvald and Nunraw Abbey west, and the mystic Traprain Law north. From the viewpoint make for the lake down the path, join with the wider path (which has run along the other side of the lake) and follow its course to the main road along Bennet's Burn. Turn left at the main road and climb the hill, following the road to the double bend, and at the second bend take the unmade field track to Meiklerig Wood (a fence has to be climbed) and on to Meiklerig Farm. Turn right and follow the established farm road to the B6370. (Please respect this as farm property where you are only a visitor.) At this main road turn left and walk into Stenton.

The central part of this delightful village, through which you are to walk, is a stretch of grass surrounded by houses hundreds of years old; note the outside stairs of the traditional Scottish split-houses. Near the village green stands the tron, or Wool Stone, on which wool was once weighed for Stenton Fair. East of the B6370 is the old Rood Well, claimed to be the best example of a medieval holy well in Scotland. The well is surmounted by fourteenth-century stonework, with a rosetted cardinal's hat on top. East Lothian has over 700 buildings of Special Architectural or Historic Interest, which include a fine range of country mansions, and of vernacular architecture, which is

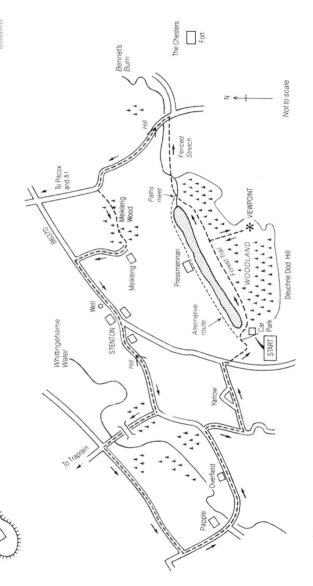

The Chesters

☐ Fort

Bennets Burn

Hill

N ←✛

Not to scale

To Pitcox and A1

Meiklerig Wood

B6370

Fenced Stretch

Paths meet

VIEWPOINT

☀

Well

Meiklerig ☐

STENTON ☐

Pressmennan

Forest Trail

WOODLAND

Deuchrie Dod Hill

Whittingehame Water

Hill

Alternative route

☐ Car Park

START

Yarrow

To Traprain

Papple

Overfield

✦✦✦ Fort ✦✦✦

☐ Fort

31

unparalleled in Scotland. At Stenton, Biel House and Ruchlaw House come into this category.

Walk through the village, keeping to the B6370, and down the hill. After about ½ mile the road bends sharply, at which point you turn right on to the minor road. Walk for about ¼ mile until you come to a bridge over the road, go under the bridge and bear left with the road over the Whittingehame Water; there is a large school property on your left. Follow this road round to Papple, past Whittingehame Mains, as far as the B6370 again. Turn left and walk along this road, via Overfield, to the junction with the road to Yarrow. Turn right into the Yarrow road, and left to Yarrow proper. Cross the bridge over the Sauchet Water and make for Ruchlaw West Mains. Turn right and this will bring you back to the track to the forest trail car park.

As you walk around the south-east borderland note the ruined towers. There is one off the road to Papple, in the woodland by the river, another south of Overfield and the shells of others nearby on this walk. From the earliest times to the seventeenth century, these towers, to which was normally attached an enclosure for service buildings known as a barmkin, were the typical homes of the lairds (Lowland dialect for landed proprietor) or lesser nobility. Border towers are colloquially called 'peels', but the peel in its proper sense was a timber palisade, such as frequently accompanied a tower in early times.

Special Interest: Traprain Law
This land was a stronghold of the Votadini tribe in prehistoric times. Here the tribesmen pursued a different life, in the main, from their pastoral orientated brothers of elsewhere in East Lothian and the Borders. The tribesmen of Traprain were metalworkers. On the top of Traprain Law was a great protected settlement, the fortifications of which can still be seen. The settlement is chiefly known as the biggest in Scotland which survived the Roman occupation. In 1919 a remarkable hoard of Gallo-Roman silver was discovered here. The treasure can now be seen in the Museum of Antiquities, Edinburgh. The Law (hill) is scalable and offers the reward of a magnificent view of East Lothian and beyond.

At the foot of the Law are the extensive ruins of Hailes Castle. It was a stronghold of the Hepburns, and it was to Hailes that the Earl of Bothwell brought Mary, Queen of Scots, during their flight from Borthwick. A portion of the east tower, a stairway and parts of the curtain wall are of the fortress built in the thirteenth century. Note the two pit-prisons.

Floors Castle, Kelso, the home of the Duke of Roxburghe (Walk 12)

Peebles, with parish church and footbridge over the river Tweed (Walk 21)

Iron age fort and broch at Edin's Hall, Berwickshire (Walk 1)

St Mary's Loch, Selkirkshire (Walk 17)

Seashore at Gullane, East Lothian (Walk 6)

St Abbs harbour
and bay,
Berwickshire
(Walk 3)

Walk 8

5 miles (8 km)

OS sheet 67

Tyninghame

This walk is through an area which is protected by legislation and is classed as 'Georgian landscape'. It is a walk for a day when you are inclined to stop and stare. The walk begins at the end of a great avenue of trees at Tyninghame, which is a short distance from the A1 road, just north of Dunbar. The land here is the last lap made by the River Tyne on its way to the North Sea and comprises some of the loveliest pastoral landscape in Scotland.

The cottages at Tyninghame, which you pass on your left as you take the A198 from the A1, are grouped around smooth squares and strips of lawn. Everywhere there are flowers and trees. Pass the village and go up the hill; the first turning on your right is Limetree Walk. The Walk itself is about a mile long; at its end go forward past the farm down a narrow road to a car park.

Out of the car park is a forked earth path; turn right here and follow the path down towards the sea. You are now walking through the heart of a preservation area named after the pioneer naturalist John Muir, who was born in 1838 at nearby Dunbar. Where the path forks, take the left-hand path and walk on to the sea. Turn left and follow the path along the shore. On your left are three great dunes, the highlight of Ravensheugh Sands. The path is clear, so make towards the outlet of the Peffer Burn at Peffer Sands. To the left are the plantation strips of Lochhouses which join onto Garleton Wood (private property). This part of the walk is particularly for the birdwatcher. The distinctive shellduck is seen here all year round, as is the black-headed gull; note that the winter feathers of the gull take on a white tinge to mask the black head, and how the young gull has just a black spot behind the eye, with two bands of black or brown tip feathers across the back. Here too you can see ringed plovers, teal and wigeon.

Retrace your steps when you come to the burn (the path goes on). As you pass the junction with the path you first came down, you pass the seaward Frances Craig. Follow the path round the headland to the cairn. At the cairn, pause and take in the sands of Tyne Mouth. The cairn is of Bronze Age date and on the shore beyond it is a cape with a rock called St Baldred's Cradle.

To the south is the well-known Belhaven Bay with its many

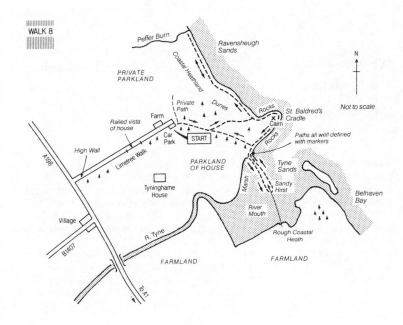

seabirds. To the north is the Bass Rock, a precipitous mass of basalt, 130ft high and about a mile in circumference. There was a castle on the rock from early times and traces of a chapel, which was connected with St Baldred, remain. After 1671 the Bass Rock was used as a prison. Across from the rock is Tantallon Castle, romantic stronghold of the Douglas family. All this land around Tyninghame was the domain of the Earls of Haddington. Facing the sea here, over Tyninghame Links is Tyninghame House, with its balustered terraces, statued gardens and well-tended pasturage. Near the house are the remains of St Baldred's twelfth-century parish church.

The walk remains gentle and uncomplicated. At the cairn follow the path round the sands and shingle of Tyne Sands, out onto the promontary known as Sandy Hirst, the predominant character of which is bracken, heath and rough grassland. The path will lead you in a loop around Sandy Hirst until it joins up with itself at the rock of the headland. Retrace your steps for a few yards, and turn left for the path to the car park.

Special Interest: Tyninghame Trees
The trees of Tyninghame have been famous for nearly 300 years, ever since the sixth Earl of Haddington, the founder of the plantation woodland in Scotland, set to work in 1705 to transform the 300-acre Muir of Tyninghame into the splendid Binning Wood. His fondness

34

for planting trees continued, until he finally resolved 'to fight no more with the cultivation of bad land, but to plant it all', even to the water's edge. He wrote thus in a letter to his grandson, 'as the oak is my favourite tree, I have planted it everywhere; and I can show them very thriving and rich, poor, middling, healthy, gravelly, clayey, mossy, spouty and rock ground, even upon dry sand.' The earl handed on to his descendants 800 acres of beautiful forest. The Binning Woods disappeared in the need for wood brought about by World War II. Today they have been replanted. The whole woodland area of Tyninghame has a wide range of coniferous and broad-leaved trees, from rowan to horse-chestnut and from beech to sycamore. The principal trees of note, however, are lime, sycamore, Scots pine and oak.

4½ miles (7 km)

OS sheet 67

This is a high-level and bracing, hilly walk, breath-catching for the first few hundred yards, with stupendous views and contours over hill and dale, forest and moor. Only one short part of it is tough walking over bracken.

First you must arrive at Spott. From the A1 Dunbar by-pass take the turning for Spott. Immediately, you enter the foothills of Lothian Edge. Go down the narrow road past Easter Broomhouse farm. It's uphill now; notice the standing stone on your left, and the closed reservoir on your right. Snake over the bridge and into Spott. Park (considerately) on the verge in the village.

The starting point is the T-junction of the road from the A1 and the road to Brunt, Woodhall and Elmscleugh (look for the Victorian cast-iron sign) off left. Walk up the tarmac road (ignoring the drive off to the right at the junction), climbing all the time, to a spot where the road bends for the second time. Pause here and take in the view over the sea, Dunbar, Berwick Law (612ft), a conical hill of felsite, and the Bass Rock. Look around for the conical farm buildings, the last remains of the horse mills. Continue up the road and pass through the gate where the road makes a sharp bend to the right. If the gate near the bend is closed on your approach, close it after you.

For the next ½ mile or so the walk is along a dead-straight half-metalled track beside a fence. From this path there is a good view across the Brunt Hill (left) and Black Law (right), the foothills of the long Lothian Edge. At the end of the track—by now you are well past the hewn plantation of Spott Dod—turn right and mount up the Chesters Hill. The path is at times a little faint but brings you up to the great fort of Chesters. The fort is on rolling ground about 400ft above the sea and is one of the best-preserved examples of multivallate (that is having three or more lines of defence) systems of prehistoric earthworks in Scotland. A first glance can show how unsound the situation of the fort was strategically, in that it is immediately under a steep scarp (an inner slope of a ditch of a fortified place) from which any lethal missile could be hurled or shot into the interior of the fort. The enclosed area measures around 12 × 5yds and is surrounded by slight traces of a ruined rampart. Another rampart surrounds this with traces of six others further out. It is likely that this fort, like others noted on these walks, underwent several phases of reconstruction

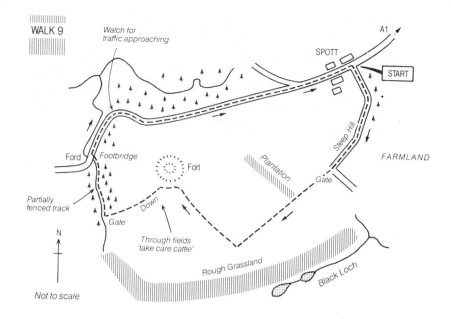

Watch for
traffic approaching

A1

SPOTT

START

Ford

Footbridge

Fort

Plantation

Steep Hill

Gate

FARMLAND

Partially
fenced track

Gate

N

Down

Through fields
'take care cattle'

Rough Grassland

Black Loch

Not to scale

with the multivallate belonging to the later phase.

From the south side of the fort, make for the apex of the wall directly in front of you. Pass through the gate and walk a few yards to where the wall, on your right, is joined by a fence leading to the plantation. Climb the wall and walk down the right-hand side of the fence (through the sheep fields) until it meets the plantation. Go down the tree-lined gulley until you meet the road. Walk right, onto the road, to the forked junction and the main road. On your left is a burn which guides you back through the small forest valley to the main road. When you arrive at the road, note the ancient ford.

The road takes you back all the way to Spott, through a delightful wooded area. Spott Mill is the first group of buildings in the trees on your left. The road is narrow so keep to the right, listening carefully at the corners and rises for oncoming traffic (which is very light).

Special Interest: Horse mills

Tourists passing through this area often remark on the characteristic architectural feature to be seen on many of the older farms. The conical buildings, often on the north and cooler side of the steading and always adjoining the barn, invariably cause puzzlement. These distinctive buildings are important relics of industrial archaeology.

Horse mills are low, circular stone buildings, with conical roofs, which used to house and protect the timber horse engine that drove the threshing drum in the adjoining barn. Generally, the horse mill has several openings and a very intricate core of roof timbers. The rafters diminish in size towards the apex of the roof in the older examples, and are clad with slates on the outside and usually finished in a simple knop finial (or weather vane). Internally the horse mill is dominated by the large square cross beam crossing the centre of the mill parallel to the barn wall. This beam was formerly used to support the central shaft of the engine. The mills were used for threshing. In 1845, 267 of the 386, 60-acre farms of East Lothian had horse mills, so there are plenty of relics to look for.

Walk 10

Eildon Hill

5 miles (8 km)

OS sheet 73

The triple peaks of the Eildon Hills stand out as a heather-matted island in a sea of rich Border farming land. They have been the home of man from the earliest times. Here early man turned a summit into a fortress, the remains of the circular fortifications of which can still be seen. (The Romans, too, knew the hills, calling them *Trimontium*, 'the three hills', and building an important fort in their foothills.)

The three conspicuous summits of Eildon (south summit 1215ft; middle 1385ft; north-east 1327ft) were once a single cone, legend tells. It is said the Scottish wizard, Michael Scot, made a demon cleft the cone into three. Again Scottish myth tells how, in a cave under the hills, the ghosts of King Arthur and his knights lie waiting to come to Britain's aid, should there be a national catastrophe. Here too, the poet Thomas the Rhymer is said to have spent more than three years in the enchanted country within the Eildons after his capture by the Queen of Elfhame, Scotland's fairyland.

From Galashiels or Selkirk follow the A7 into Melrose, following signs for the Abbey. From the south, take the A68 into Newtown St Boswells, then fork left onto the A6091 which will bring you right to the beginning of the walk.

Park in the free car park, and start the Eildon walk at the old railway station (once on the Carlisle-Edinburgh line, but now closed) at Melrose, off the B6359, following the signs for Lilliesleaf from the town centre. From the car park walk straight ahead until the main road is reached, and then turn right up the hill. On reaching the gap between the houses on the left-hand side, turn down the steps and follow the signs marked 'Eildon Walk'. Cross over the stile and follow the right-hand margin of the field.

About halfway up the field a viewpoint gives the first fine glimpse of Melrose. The little medieval town spreads over the level ground between the foot of the Eildon Hills and the river Tweed. It has a market cross dating from 1642 and Greenyards, the famous rugby ground where the seven-a-side version of the game originated. Once at the top edge of the field pass through a gate and then over a stile; follow the path round the left-hand edge of the field, over another stile, and continue straight ahead over open ground to follow the well marked path between gorse bushes to the saddle of the hills.

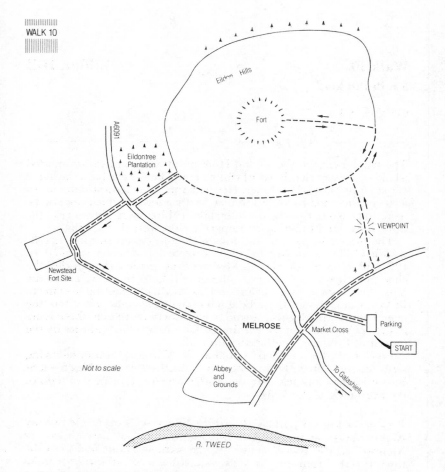

Eildon Hills

Fort

A6091

Eildon tree
Plantation

VIEWPOINT

Newstead
Fort Site

MELROSE

Market Cross

Parking

START

Not to scale

Abbey
and
Grounds

To Galashiels

R. TWEED

On the saddle between the hills, turn right onto a broader path up to the summit of Eildon Hill North. From the summit are splendid views in every direction, extending to the Cheviot Hills in the south, the Lammermuirs in the north and the hills of Galloway towards the south-west. To Sir Walter Scott the hills served as romantic inspiration. From here he could look over at the land he loved and wrote about. 'I can', he noted, 'stand on Eildon Hill and point out forty-three places famous in war and verse.'

The steep slopes of Eildon are the home of a wide range of birdlife, from kestrels and meadow pipits on the heights to stonechats, whinchats and wheatears on the wooded lower slopes. Cattle here are mostly Herefords, Friesians and Aberdeen Angus, sharing the land with Blackface rams and Cheviot sheep.

40

Come back down the hill where the path directly descending to Melrose makes a fork. Then follow the path round the edge of the hill, keeping to the belt above the trees. The path then angles sharply down to a main road. On the right, before the road is reached, one can see the Eildontree plantation, which takes its name from the Eildon Tree on the north side of the plantation. The tree is famous for its mention in the ballad *Thomas the Rhymer*.

Turn sharp right along the main road (A6091 to Kelso) and walk for about 100yds, then take a sharp left turn along the hedge farm road. At the T-junction after the old railway bridge, turn left at the 'Melrose' sign. Keep left up the road for around 50yds, and on your left will be the Roman fort of Newstead. The fort was built in about AD 80 and finally abandoned a century later.

When you arrive opposite Dean Cottages, turn left through the gate of the riding school. Keep to the left of the stables and follow the narrow path behind bungalows and along the edge of the embankment. Follow the paved way past the houses to the road then keep right down the hill. On your left will be the fields called the Annay, leading to the river, thence to the abbey.

Melrose Abbey won international fame through the works of Sir Walter Scott. Founded in 1136 by King David I, the abbey was built for Cistercian monks from Rievaulx, Yorkshire. Under the patronage of the kings of Scotland the abbey grew rich and powerful. The monks were known for their skills as sheep farmers and fruit growers. Because of its position the abbey was the object of constant attack; it never recovered from the assault in 1545 by the Earl of Hertford. Its ruins date mostly from the fifteenth century and house the buried heart of King Robert the Bruce. In the abbey grounds is the sixteenth-century fortified Commendator's House, which is now a museum.

From the abbey road turn onto the main road. To the left is the Market Cross leading back to Lilliesleaf road and the railway station.

Special Interest: Mercat Cross
Once every town of importance in Scotland had its Mercat Cross, the name deriving from the old Scottish word for 'market'. The cross at Melrose is dated 1642 and bears the arms of Scotland. The cross has been a popular meeting point for centuries. From here the members of the ancient Masonic Lodge of Melrose march by torchlight to the abbey on 27 December (St John's Day). This ceremony dates back to 1746.

41

This walk sets off to a fine degree the famous River Tweed, one of the largest rivers in the British Isles, which contains some 16 species of fish. Because of its importance in terms of hydrology and biology, the complete basin of the Tweed has been designated a site of Special Scientific Interest. The Tweed rises in the Tweedsmuir Hills in south-west Peeblesshire and flows in a north-easterly direction to enter the North Sea at Berwick-upon-Tweed. It drains an area of 1,870 square miles, and is best known for its salmon fishing. The river is only navigable for the last 6 miles of its 97-mile length.

Depending on the season, of course, the walker here may see the salmon fishermen fishing from boats on various stretches of the river. The Tweed is divided into well-defined fishing areas called beats, each of which has a local name. The boatmen all know these beats by heart and act as 'gillies' to visiting anglers.

Present day Newtown St Boswells lies some distance to the north of St Boswells, which was the original settlement founded by St Boisil, a monk from the nearby monastery at Old Mailros. Its village green is the scene of a Fair each July. Centuries ago, the Fair attracted dealers from all over Britain to sell sheep, cattle and horses. Here too 'muggers' (the old name for 'hawkers', and nothing to do with the unfortunate modern meaning) sold all kinds of crockery.

From Kelso take the A699 to Newtown St Boswells; from Selkirk, the A699 (west); from Galashiels and Melrose, the A7 and the A6091. From the north and the south, the A68 passes through Newtown St Boswells.

Park safely at the village green or in the side streets, or where directed to do so if you visit during Fair time.

The start of the walk is in the heart of Newtown St Boswells, and the exact position can be found at the bus stop opposite the Royal Bank of Scotland. From here walk along Melbourne Place past the Post Office, and follow the road away to the left signposted 'To the Glen'. This road changes to a track as it gently descends past the sewage works (no need to increase walking speed!) to a small footbridge over a burn.

This wooded glen is a fine example of the semi-natural woodland of

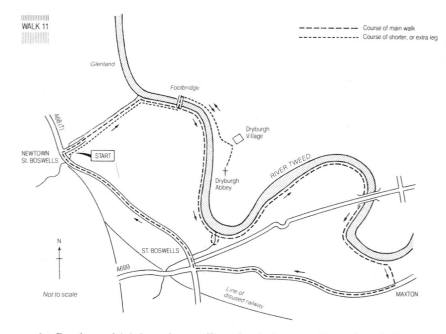

WALK 11

Glenland

Footbridge

Dryburgh
Village

A68(T)

NEWTOWN
St. BOSWELLS

START

RIVER TWEED

Dryburgh
Abbey

N

ST. BOSWELLS

A699

Not to scale

Line of
disused railway

MAXTON

------- Course of main walk
--------- Course of shorter, or extra leg

the Borders which have been affected only in a small way by 'civilisa-
tion'. Because of its diversity and layout, the glen has well over 120
species of plants. In season look for the bladder campion, the bird's-
foot trefoil and the greater celandine. Herein too are many different
types of bird life, from blackcap and willow warbler, to chiffchaff and
tawny owl.

Cross the footbridge and follow the path straight ahead until it
eventually rises, by a series of steps, to a viewpoint above the River
Tweed. Then descend the steep path to the road where there is a
footbridge to the left. This footbridge leads across the Tweed to
Dryburgh and the abbey. As the abbey and the village are in a cul-de-
sac bend of the river, this may be taken as an extra leg to the walk. Go
over the bridge, turn right and follow the road into the village and
thence to the abbey and its grounds—well worth a visit.

Assuming that you have now been to the abbey, or decided not to
go, pass the footbridge and walk down the rough track, turning off
right through the trees. Walk, now, along the side of the Tweed for
about a mile. At the foot of the gulley, below the town of (Old) St
Boswells, the path climbs to the right up to the town. At the top of this
path, follow the marked route to the houses and down to the Golf
Course. Walk, now, to the end of the Golf Course and a stile. Climb
the stile and follow the path by the river to Mertoun bridge. Across the
river is Mertoun House, once the home of the Earls of Ellesmere.

43

At the bridge climb to the road, cross the road and descend to the path by the river. Continue along the sloped bank (known in Scotland as a 'haugh') to a stile at the edge of a plantation. Climb the stile and follow the path through the wood, passing the well below Benrig House, to steps beside the wall. Climb the steps and at the top turn left, following the path beside the graveyard. The path descends, crosses the burn by a wooden footbridge and climbs through the wood to Maxton Church. At the church follow the paved path onto the road and take the fork right up into Maxton village. Maxton retains the shaft of its old cross and the church is of twelfth-century foundation. Look away to the right and see Penielheugh, a monument to the Battle of Waterloo.

At the centre of the village the walker can take the most direct route back to Newtown St Boswells, namely the A699. At the crossroads turn right up the A68 (T), via St Boswells, back to the start of the walk. The disused railway will be on your left all the way from Maxton.

Special Interest: Dryburgh Abbey
Dryburgh was the site selected in 1140 by the Canons Regular of the Premonstratensian Order for their first home in Scotland, under the sponsorship of Hugh de Morville, Lord of Lauderdale. On the site of the abbey was the sixth-century sanctuary of St Modan. Being close to the Border, the abbey fell foul of English raiding parties many times. In 1322 and in 1385 it was ruined by the English and rebuilt, but after a more complete destruction by the Earl of Hertford in 1544, it seems never to have been rebuilt. The abbey is famous as the last resting place of Sir Walter Scott and Earl Haig, of World War I fame. Note too the quaint, but appealing, memorial built in 1749 by David, Earl of Buchan, in honour of his ancestors. Recessed into one side of an obelisk is an approximately life-sized statue of James I with drawn sword, and bearing a plumed hat. On the reverse is James IV.

Note: This walk is now on a bus route. So a bus (from Kelso) can be taken from Maxton to Newtown St Boswells. Alternatively, take the bus to Maxton and walk the river route to Newtown St Boswells via Dryburgh. In high summer the Maxton/St Boswells road is very busy with coaches, so take care.

Walk 12   Kelso

7½ miles (12·5 km)

OS sheet 74

Kelso is a town of airy streets with well-built houses having walls of pale clean stone and roofs of ink-blue slate. Known in the twelfth century as Calkou ('Chalkheugh'), the subsequent town has been the butt of many raids by English invaders, and has known armies as varied as those of James III to Bonnie Prince Charlie. A walk round the town is worth a separate venture, to savour its generous square and 'air' of a continental town.

Kelso Abbey was founded by King David I in 1128, having been settled by Tironesian monks from Selkirk. The abbey suffered much spoliation because of war, and was badly damaged by English raiders in 1542, 1544 and 1545. Only a portion of the west end of the abbey remains, where James III, at the age of eight, was crowned King of Scotland.

The walk begins at a free car park called The Knowes, which is reached by a lane called The Putts, from the town square, via Wood Market. The car park is spacious, free of charge, and supplied with public conveniences. From the car park head towards the ruined abbey tower along a path called Abbey Walk. On your right will be the old parish church, built in 1773 and much altered in 1823 and 1833, and a 'reclaimed' graveyard which has now been made into a park. At the end of this walkway is the abbey.

In front of the abbey is a crossroads. Bear left round the abbey walking into Bridge Street. A few yards along on the right is the War Memorial made up of mock cloisters. Walk on until you come to the bridge over the River Tweed, and cross, so that you are alongside the right-hand parapet. This five-arched bridge was built in 1803 to the design of John Rennie, FRS, who used it as a model for his Waterloo Bridge on the Thames. Cross the bridge and turn right along the A699; Springwood Park will be on your left.

Follow the road along the west bank of the River Tweed, continuing left alongside the River Teviot, a river which rises on the Dumfriesshire border 36 miles away. Cross Teviot Bridge and walk to a stile in the wall on the left-hand side of the road past the cottage. Climb the stile and follow the path down the riverside and past Roxburgh Castle.

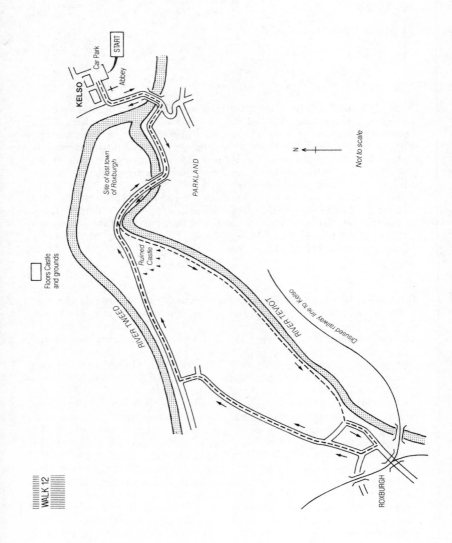

WALK 12

KELSO

Floors Castle and grounds

RIVER TWEED

Site of lost town of Roxburgh

Ruined Castle

PARKLAND

RIVER TEVIOT

Disused railway line to Kelso

ROXBURGH

Car Park

Abbey

START

N

Not to scale

Once 'the jewel of Roxburgh town', the castle was the birthplace of Alexander III. Water fowl are common sights all along this stretch of the river, but look for them particularly at Hogarth's Mill, opposite the junction of the Tweed and the Teviot. Large numbers of tufted duck, goldeneye, wigeon and coot gather to feed on the grain around the mill. At the river junction salmon can be seen jumping during the autumn and spring spawning runs. Below the ruins of Roxburgh Castle, the greater spotted woodpecker, kingfisher and heron have all been observed. Watch out for the dangers of giant hogweed.

The path continues along the west bank of the River Teviot for $1\frac{1}{2}$ miles, until it joins the road into Roxburgh Village via a stile above Roxburgh Mill Farm. Climb the stile and follow the road to the left into the village. In the village bear right to the fork and turn sharp right at the old, disused, railway viaduct. Follow this road round and a few yards past the farm of Roxburgh Barns is the junction with the A699. Turn right and follow the road back into Kelso.

On your left will be Floors Castle, built in 1721 by William Adam in the style of Vanburgh, and later added to by Playfair. It is the home of the Duke of Roxburghe. In the castle grounds is the holly tree marking the spot where James II was killed by an exploding cannon. The fields running down to the river are now called Vigorous Haugh and the river islands below the weir, Back Bullers.

Special Interest: The lost town of Roxburgh

The lost town of Roxburgh, sited where the flat fields now roll down to the rivers, was once a Royal Burgh and capital of Scotland. Of the old Royal Burgh little remains to be seen, but look for the carved stone or two among the trees, a tell-tale hump of the ruins of its castle. You are privileged, for few who pass today know that the town ever existed. Founded, it is thought, by David I (1124–53), the town was a centre of culture in a land of barbarity. Here the king dispensed the law from his court and sponsored a Royal Mint. Schools and churches sprang up within its walls. The king also encouraged religious orders to set up foundations in the town, with a hospital run by ecclesiastics.

Merchants flourished at Roxburgh. Here was the only bridge over the Tweed beyond Berwick and, as the fords on the river were notoriously unsafe, Roxburgh became the crossroads for commerce. By the time Alexander III became king, in 1249, Roxburgh was by far the largest and most important town in Scotland.

With the development of Scotland's maritime trade, Roxburgh declined, and by the sixteenth century it had become a sinister ghost town, and a quarry for the new town of Kelso was set up on the other side of the river. Today, the lost town of Roxburgh cries out for excavation; from time to time bits of carved stone, bones, jewellery and statuary come to light here.

Walk 13   Craik Forest

3¼ miles (5 km)

OS sheet 79

Although a comparatively short walk, this one has a rich variety of things to see and savour. Craik Forest lies between the Ettrick and Borthwick valleys and is close to extensive areas of private forestry plantations. Because the ground here is of high exposure and is poorly drained, with peat or heavy clay soil, a range of hardy trees are all that may be grown. The main species of tree to be seen are Sitka and Norway spruce, with some larch and pine. In sheltered situations there are some less hardy conifers and broadleaved trees. The great proportion of the trees cut here go to pulp mills.

The best way to get to this walk is via Hawick, which is reached by taking the A698 from Kelso, or the A7 from Selkirk. Take the A7 out of Hawick, to the south and turn off to the right along the B711 Roberton road. Just beyond Roberton village take the road to Borthwick Water for around 6 miles; this leads to a car park near the Forest Office at the beginning of the walk.

Starting in the car park, walk through the policy woods. You will see that a great many of the older trees have been felled, but scores of young saplings have been planted and labelled for easy identification. Bear left at the T-junction and follow the boundary of the plantation above the stream called Aithouse Burn. The open fields of Craik Farm will be on your right and facing east.

After a short while you will come to a main forest road to Craik near a concrete bridge, from here keep following the Aithouse Burn path. Around this area you ought to begin to notice that the wildlife is abundant on this walk; keep a sharp look out for wildlife, especially along the margin of the water's edge and at the openings of the plantations. Of the mammals to be seen, roe deer, hares, badgers, foxes and rabbits are most common. A deer ranger walks this forest to protect, care for and carry out a planned control programme for the deer. In the forest there is a wide variety of bird life. Kestrels, short-eared owls, grouse, partridges and pheasants are frequently seen in the newer plantations. The older woodlands are the favourite haunts of thrushes, pigeons, wrens, tits and finches.

Keep following the burn for a further ½ mile or so, turning left (west) up Wolfcleuch Burn to the waterfall. Here stretches out an open

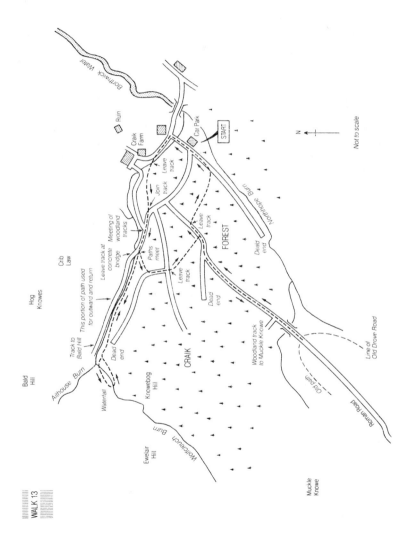

WALK 13

Borthwick Water

Run

Craik Farm

Car Park

START

Northridge Burn

N

Not to scale

Crib Law

Hog Knowes

Join
Leave track

Leave track

Meeting of woodland tracks

Leave track at concrete bridge

Paths meet

Leave track

FOREST

Dead end

Dead end

This portion of path used for outward and return

Bald Hill

Track to Bald Hill

Aithouse Burn

Dead end

Waterfall

Knowebog Hill

CRAIK

Woodland track to Muckle Knowe

Line of Old Drove Road

Old path

Roman Road

Ewelair Hill

Wolfcleuch Burn

Muckle Knowe

49

grassy area ideal for resting, meditating, or just staring. You are now between Knowebog Hill and Ewelair Hill.

The return route from the waterfall takes the path down the opposite side of the burn and rejoins the outward route of the walk after about ¼ mile. Walk from here to the point where a well-defined path branches off to the right (west). Climb the bank and pass through an area where the trees have been cleared after a severe wind-blow (the area has been replanted). You now come to a main forest track. Follow this for a few yards and out through where the track joins another at a T-junction. Walk along this path until you come to another forest track; turn right and follow the track until it forks, taking the left fork. Continue walking until you cross a bridge. Just over the bridge, and forking right, is the line of the old Roman Road. Branching to the left is also an old drove road past Kidds Scar.

When you have looked at, and maybe traced, some of the length of the ancient road, retrace your steps, to where you first joined this forest track. Walk for a short way down the track past the joining point and cut down right. Follow a long straight path to the valley bottom where there is an attractive picnic area. The car park is two or three minutes walk from the picnic area.

Special Interest: Drove roads and Roman roadway
Craik Forest is crossed by a number of old drove roads. Two of these are of note; both come from East Buccleuch, one making for Hawick and the other for Teviothead. Here, too, is a Roman road which commenced at Newstead, passed through the southern part of the forest and over Craik Cross Hill into Eskdalemuir. Make a close examination of the remains of the road and see the considerable engineering expertise, in choice of materials and handling the route, which was used in its construction. Within Craik Forest the road has been preserved as a walk or ride. In places the road is difficult to define, but walk away to the side and looking across it you will see its line more easily.

Here, we are on the very frontier of Scotland and England, where the pastoral country affords great views over the Border to England's lovely Cheviots. The two villages of Yetholm, prefixed Town and Kirk respectively, are still tranquil in a bustling agricultural land. This area was once the 'Capital of the Gipsies' and is now well-known as the northern end of the Pennine Way. The Pennine Way, incidentally, goes east from Kirk Yetholm across the Halter Burn and up over the south shoulder of Green Humbleton to the ridge which forms the line of the Border; then it follows the Border over White Law, Black Hag (1,801ft) and The Schil (1,985ft) to Auchope Cairn (2,382ft). The Pennine Way diverges here to take the Cheviot (2,676ft) and returns to the Border ridge south-west to Dere Street and the Roman camps at Chew Green (See Walk 30).

The walk starts at the village of Town Yetholm. This is ¼ mile west of Kirk Yetholm on the B6401. Park in the village in the region of the open green sward of the village square. Walk along the top side of the square and bear right at the fork (the B6401 to Morebattle descends to your left). Continue on this road until you come to the first main turning right; go down this road past the T-junction on your right and keep walking forward. Follow the road to a sharp left bend then along to the pump on the left and follow the road right. Just past the buildings by a belt of trees the road becomes unfenced. You are now walking up towards Tod Craigs; ignore the two hill paths which climb away to your left. On your far left is the summit of Yetholm Law.

This track is now straight, apart from one bend by the plantation on the right, and takes you down to the Loch of Yetholm. Turn left on to the track when you come to the loch, and skirt the water following the western foot-slopes of Tod Craigs. When you have reached the end of the loch, a burn snakes south to Primside through a marshy area. Keep to the footpath which joins a minor road after a few hundred yards, bringing you down to the B6401. This latter stretch of footpath and minor road traces the boundary of the old parishes here.

Turn left at the main road and keep left at the fork for Primsidemill, passing the milestone (Kelso 8/Cocklawfoot 7). Although this road is the main road between Mindrum and Morebattle, it formed one

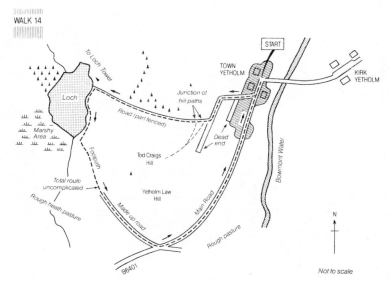

of the old 'kirk' roads. The hills of this area are full of lost villages—there's one at Clifton, if you follow the Primsidemill road—ruined chapels and forts. A 'kirk' road, of course, was the right of way local inhabitants had to carry their coffins to the churchyards in the villages.

You return to your starting point of the walk following the west bank of the Bowmont Water. Across the river on the right is Duncanhaugh, Hayhope and the ancient quarries of Staerough Hill.

Special Interest: Capital of the Gipsies

No one knows when the gipsies first came to Scotland and settled in Yetholm. Yet, as long ago as the fifteenth century, state papers record bands of strange vagrants infiltrating from over the Border. A writ of James V in 1540 refers to Johnne Faw, 'Lord and Erle of Litill Egypt'. He was one of the gipsies' 'royal house' of Faa who held court at Yetholm, and lorded it over the tribes who wandered through the Border country. The dignitaries among these gipsies were known as Lords and Erles.

The most famous Yetholm gipsy was Jean Gordon (she was to become Meg Merriles in Sir Walter Scott's book *Guy Mannering*). Jean Gordon was a great character and passed on her eccentricities to her grand-daughter Madge, a six-foot tanned gipsy lass known for her outrageous straw bonnets. Jean Gordon became the wife of Patrick Faa and by him had four sons; three of them and their wives were hanged for sheep-stealing at Jedburgh in 1730. You can still see the home of Esther Faa Blythe, last Queen of the Gipsies. Her cottage is still known as the 'Palace'. A great crowd gathered here in 1883 to attend Esther's funeral and witness the end of the gipsy dynasty.

Walk 15

6¼ miles (10 km)

OS sheet 73

Abbotsford

This walk through the heart of one of Scotland's great literary heritages—Walter Scott country—has no complications. It begins and ends in the former burgh of Galashiels which stands on the Gala Water, close to its meeting with the River Tweed. The earliest inhabitants here were Britons, speaking a tongue from which Welsh and Cornish are derived. In Roman times this land was a part of the territory of the Votadini tribe, and maybe by the fifth and sixth centuries, it was possibly the kingdom of the Gododdin, which was displaced by that of the Angle invaders of the ninth century.

For centuries Galashiels—the name comes from the ancient British *gwala* 'a full stream' and the Anglo-Saxon *shiel* 'a temporary herdsman's shelter'—was the tiny village giving shelter to pilgrims on the way to Melrose Abbey. Galashiels is now a little industrial town famous for its tweeds. English walkers may care to note that the word 'tweed' has nothing to do with the River Tweed. It comes from a clerical error. An English clerk wrote the Scots word 'tweels', meaning woollen fabric, as 'tweeds', and the name has stuck ever since.

To arrive at Galashiels from the north take the A7 from Edinburgh, via Dalkeith; from the south and east, the A7 and the A6091 via Melrose and St Boswells; from the south, take the A7 from Selkirk. (To avoid confusion, the A7 takes a double loop south of Galashiels, so that part goes on to Darnlee and part veers off to Selkirk, forming a bypass.)

Begin the walk at the car park in Livingstone Place, and turn right into Scott Street. Walk down Scott Street, past the junction with St John Street on the left and into Scott Crescent. On your right will be the gates of Scott Park. The large old-fashioned house on your left is Old Gala House, once the home of the Laird of Gala. The present house, which grew from the small wing on the south-east, dates from around 1583 and has additions from subsequent centuries. The garden in which it stands is all that remains of the orchards and parks which used to be there.

Walk past the old house and follow the road as it bends to a crossroads; on your left will be Lawyers Brae and on the right Elm

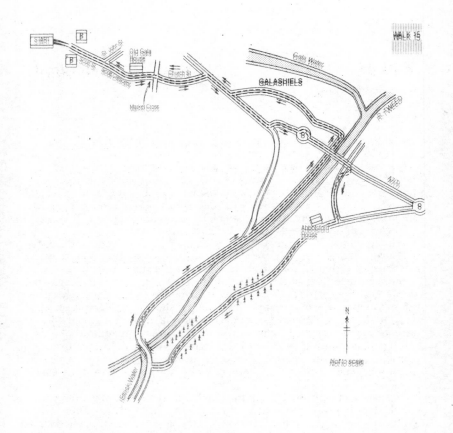

Row. Here was where the ancient Mercat Cross stood, site of annual fairs, where criminals were whipped, weekly markets were held and proclamations were read. The cross seen today was erected in 1695 and restored in 1887. At the cross each year in early June, during the 'Braw Lads Gathering', the ceremony of the 'Mingling of the Roses' takes place to commemorate King James IV's grant, of the lordship of nearby Ettrick Forest, to his English bride Margaret Tudor in 1503.

Cross the Market Cross concourse and enter Church Street ahead. The building on the corner of Elm Row and Scott Crescent was the old Cloth Hall, built by the Manufacturers' Corporation in the eighteenth century for the storage and sale of woollen cloth. Carry on down Church Street, through the Church Square housing development to the main Selkirk road (A7). Follow this road past the roundabout down to the bridge over the River Tweed.

Below the bridge was the town's old Ford; from the bridge are fine views of the Selkirk side of the Tweed (right) and Galashiels/Melrose side of the Tweed (left). Cross over the bridge on the right-hand side and descend to the path by the river. A few yards from the old ford crossing, walk up the hill to where the track meets the B6360. Turn right and continue up this road. At the brow of the hill you will see the car park on your left; on the right is the tourist gateway down into Abbotsford House. Pass the car park and walk on the grass verges. This road has high bankings for a goodly part of its length; an ideal place to search for hedgerow flowers like the prickly sow thistle and the bush vetch. Some of the roadside trees hereabouts exhibit some interesting fungi; look for the distinctive Jew's ear fungus, the beefsteak fungus and the honey fungus; the latter appearing at the base of trees.

As you walk down this road, Cauldshiels Hill and Loch are up on your left; famous in legend for their associations with fairy-lore. A mile or so past the second gateway down to Abbotsford House, are the gates to Faldonside House; from where the road snakes away through woodland glades to its junction with the A7 (T).

At the junction turn right and cross the new bridge. On your right sparkles the River Tweed. As the Tweed comes closer to the road, watch for the minor road off to the right which forms a delightful riverside walk back to the bridge at Galashiels, past the rear of Abbotsford House across the river. Take this minor road and follow it straight along to the town side of the old ford and the bridge.

Pass under the bridge at Galashiels, turning first left once you have walked under the bridge. Follow the road, past the hospital, to its junction with the A7. Cross the road and walk on the left-hand side. Watch for the Church Street junction on the left, for, by walking back up Church Street and Scott Crescent, you will arrive safely back at the car parks in Scott Street.

If you have time, walk down St John Street into Cornmill Square and have a look at the heart of this little industrial town. In the square is Sir Robert Lorimer's ornamental fountain, which stands on the site of the town's old cornmill. See, too, the statue of the Reiver, now one of the best-known images of the Borders. (A *reiver*, in old Scots, was a robber or freebooter.)

NB: In high summer the B6360 and the A7 can be very busy. Take care to observe all traffic movements.

Special Interest: Abbotsford House

This was the home of Sir Walter Scott (1771–1832) for over 20 years. He bought the original farm, called Cartleyhole, in 1811 from Dr Robert Douglas, parish minister of Galashiels, for 4,000 guineas. Sir Walter greatly enlarged the house (pulling down the original farm house) between 1818 and 1824. The house, still lived in by members of his family, is now a literary shrine to his name and is open to the public as a museum.

Walk 16

Huntly Covert

4¼ miles (7 km)

OS sheet 73

The ancient burgh of Selkirk stands high above the Ettrick valley, 3 miles below the meeting of the waters of Ettrick and Yarrow. The burgh was ancient even in 1113, when Earl David (later David I, King of Scots) founded the abbey of Selkirk, and became the capital of Ettrick Forest, where kings came to hunt. As you stand at the heart of the burgh, in the Market Place by the statue of Sir Walter Scott, who was Sheriff of Selkirk for 33 years, there is no hint that the populace was once hit by gold fever.

Arrive at the beginning of this walk by taking the B7009 from Selkirk, turn left at the fork for Hartwoodmyres, and turn left again for the holdings. Park where the minor road becomes unfenced and the path climbs up to the Huntly Rig from Hartwoodmyres. Although the path is easily traceable, the going is rough and a jaunt for good weather. Much of the walk can be very wet after rain and remains largely unwalked in modern times, yet it has much to offer.

Take, then, the footpath from Hartwoodmyres past the summit of the triangulation pillar of Huntly Rig. This is a 2½ft high concrete pillar, painted white, used in distance and height measurement. (It has a brass plate with map reading information.) You are steadily climbing among moorland scenery to Huntly Covert, straight ahead. As you approach the covert, the footpath forks; to the left is the path leading eventually to Fanns, while the right fork leads to Hutlerburn Hill. Take the right fork, as on this way you will pass Huntly Covert on your left. As you walk you have good views of the moorland burns and the distant hills, like Caver's Hill and Shaw's Hill. Keep a look out, too, all the way, for the scars left on the countryside by the gold prospectors.

Continue along this footpath and you will see Hutlerburn Loch on your right, a nice example of a 'lost' Border loch. Walk on and you will meet an ancient track which stretches all the way from Hutlerburn down to Easter Essenside and its fine loch. The track (Hutlerburn Track) takes its name from the Hutler Burn, a tributary of the Woll Burn, which flows down, right, from your path.

Turn right at the meeting of the ways and you are cutting across the summit of Hutlerburn Hill. It is a bleak place, the haunt of a surpris-

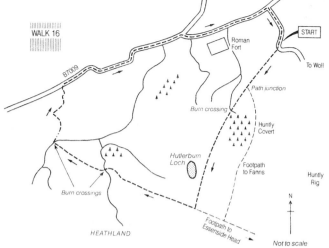

ing range of moorland birds. Look for the burn which will appear at its source on your right, this leads you down to the wood opposite Hungry Hill; it's downhill all the way now to the road. Soon your path extends between two burns. Cross the left-hand burn and tramp over Hungry Hill. Pause and look at the valley of the Ettrick Water spread out below. To the far left is Ettrickbridge and centre left Brockhill, over the Ettrick Water.

The old track descends and you follow a burn for a few yards. Cross the burn and follow the path which takes you to the road, via two sharp right-angled turns at the foot of Hawford Hill. At the road turn right (it is the B7009 Selkirk to Langholm road and can be quite busy in high summer). Walk along this road for about ½ mile, through Hutlerburn, and take the minor road right to Inner Huntly. Walk on and just past the great belt of wood on your left, you will see the last remaining L-shaped ditch of a Roman Fort, one of the link forts from Newstead to the west. Follow the road past the fort to the junction (right) up to where you parked at Hartwoodmyres.

Special Interest: The Scottish goldhunters

In the sixteenth century, people would gather at the market place of Selkirk to watch the hirings of labourers to seek gold in the Selkirkshire hills. Gold was used for coins in Scotland as early as the fourteenth century and explorations for the metal were quite widespread in the hills of Yarrow and Ettrick. Robert Seton, a Scot who had visited the gold mines of Mexico, claimed that there was gold 'about Huntlie Riggs', in the book on prospecting that he wrote in the fifteenth century. The period 1511 to 1603 appears to have been the time when most gold prospecting and discovery seems to have gone on in Scotland. Rights of gold prospecting were granted in 1593 by James VI to his banker Thomas Foullis, the Edinburgh goldsmith and erstwhile master of the Scottish Mint.

Yarrow is a mysterious vale concealed by Bowerhope Law and Watch Law, and sister laws of the Ettrick hills. Its centrepiece is St Mary's Loch, which lies at the head of the Vale of the River Yarrow, the largest loch in the south of Scotland. Three miles long, it retains its unexpressible tranquillity which spills over into its pendant Loch of the Lowes. Although a much visited area, for the most part this walk—which has a 1½-mile 'tough stretch' of moorland walking—is quiet and delightful as a typical south of Scotland lochland dale. Those enthusiasts who have read Sir Walter Scott's description of St Mary's Loch in *Marmion* will be eager to visit this land of romance.

Ideally this walk should be done in clear weather for the views of their kind are unsurpassed. Smooth-soled shoes or sandals could be dangerous as the walk has a fairly steep ascent and descent in its middle. There are several wet patches which should be carefully avoided. The moorland of the walk has free access, but consideration for the hill sheep is a must (particularly during lambing). Bridge End Hill's sunny side is good for a picnic.

St Mary's Loch is best reached by taking the A708 from Selkirk, via Yarrow.

The start of the walk is at Tibbie Shiel's Inn, now famous the world over as the name of the widow hostess Tibbie Shiel (Isabella Richardson), synonymous with good cheer and convivial evenings, immortalized in the writings and gossip of Border authors like Roberts Chambers, William Ayton and John Wilson. Tibbie died in 1878, in her 96th year and now lies in Ettrick Churchyard. The parking area around the inn tends to be full in high summer. If so, the verges of the nearby road to Crosscleugh are convenient *if carefully used*, and there is an official car park across the bridge.

From the door of Tibbie Shiel's Inn, turn west and cross the bridge. In front of you is the monument to 'The Ettrick Shepherd'. Turn right at the bridge and, keeping to the right-hand verge of the road, follow the west shore of St Mary's Loch. At the beginning and the middle of this section of the road to Cappercleugh there are two belts of mixed conifers. Walk on past the buildings and over the Summerhope Burn. Soon the road hugs close to the waters edge, and past the escarpment

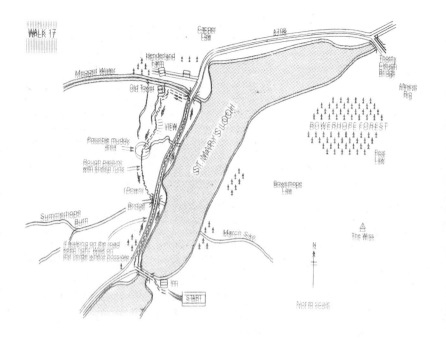

on your left is the ancient estate of Rodono, now a hotel. The estate takes its name from the barony of Rodono, which comprised the valley of the Megget Water, lands granted to the monks of Melrose Abbey in 1236.

On past the estate the road veers round to the bridge at Cappercleuch. Go to the bridge, and turn down the footpath at the left-hand side of the bridge, along the side of the Megget Water. This is on the line of the old path made by the monks of Melrose on foot to the ford at Syart and the fishing streams of Inch, Roddie and Syart. Across the water on your right are the vestiges of the old Tower of Henderland. Here lived the freebooter (robber and bandit), Piers Cockburn, who was hung from the tower gateway in 1529 by the soldiers of James V. To the far right is Capper Law and Henderland Hill.

Following the line of the Megget Water, the path rises gently and forks near its end, just before the bridge to Henderland. Take the left-hand fork and follow the path to the burn. At the burn turn left and follow the water course upwards to its birth in the foothills of Bridge End Hill. The path is rather tiring as it rises, but take your time and have plenty of rests if necessary. Keep a look out for the wet areas which can be distinguished by the brighter green grass. At the end of the burn walk straight forward towards the crest of Bridge End Hill. An excellent place to pause for breath and admire the scenery.

Look across from Bridge End Hill, towards Tibbie Shiel's Inn, and you will see a burn flowing down into St Mary's Loch at Rodono Hotel. Cross the shoulder of the hill and descend towards the burn, making towards its source. There's a path here, but the heather and grass tufts encroach quickly. The hill gets steeper, but levels off as you round the source of the burn. From the source look forward to the larger Summerhope Burn and the roadway, make for where the two meet at the bridge. The path branches and re-branches to the sheep's will, but it makes no difference which path you choose. Take your time to savour the view. Directly in front, across the loch, are Bowerhope Law (left), The Wiss (right) and the forest of Bowerhope. At the bridge by the road, turn right and retrace your steps to Tibbie Shiel's Inn.

Special Interest: The Ettrick Shepherd

The Ettrick Shepherd is the name by which the writer James Hogg is best known. Born at Ettrick in 1770, he was employed as a herdsman from almost his earliest days and had little education. Stirred by the example of Burns, he became a voracious reader of poetry and began to write himself. In 1801 he published his *Scottish Pastorals*. His popular works include *The Mountain Bard* and *The Shepherd's Guide*, but he is perhaps more prominently known as the author of the macabre novel *The Private Memoirs and Confessions of a Justified Sinner* (1824), and *Domestic Memoirs and Private Life of Sir Walter Scott* (1834).

Hogg died in 1835, and the monument you see shows him sitting on an oak root, grasping his shepherd's staff and holding a scroll bearing the words 'He taught the wandering winds to sing' (the last line of his *The Queen's Wake*, 1813); verses from the same work are on the panels of the pedestal. Incidentally, as a girl Tibbie Shiel was in service to Hogg's mother.

Walk 18

White Meldon Settlements

5½ miles (9 km)

OS sheet 73

This walk is good for leg-stretching, rising through heathland to open moor, moorland tracks, Roman road and where there are the remains of ancient Iron Age settlements and forts. There are good views on the way and you are likely to see few people but many moorland birds. For the most part walking is easy, but one section does require tough walking shoes. A tube of insect repellent in the pocket is an added comfort in high summer (not just for this walk, of course).

Take the A72 from Peebles to Biggar. Turn right, up the road, for White Meldon; pass Meldon Cottage and Green Knowe plantation is 1½ miles onward.

The walk starts at the public convenience at Green Knowe plantation. The first 1½ miles of the walk is along established, tarred, minor road which is fenced. One third of this stretch is flanked by Green Knowe plantation on your left (for you are proceeding in the opposite direction to that of your arrival). You are walking between two hills, Black Meldon and White Meldon (on your right), both crowned by extensive Iron Age forts, of which the White Meldon one has double ditches. Almost level with the end of Green Knowe plantation, on the right, is a settlement of seven Iron Age enclosures, first the Harehope Burn, then the Meldon Burn. Walk on until you come to a fork right. As you walk along you can broom- and gorse-spot. Note that broom has five-angled, non-prickly stems whereas gorse has pea-like flowers and prickles. Confusion arises because both have yellow flowers. This is the land too of the petty whin with its wiry stems and oval leaves.

Follow the minor road, in part unfenced, to Upper Kidston; the road is straight and good walking. At the end of the road to Upper Kidston, about 2½ miles from the turning, an old track cuts across the modern holdings right to left, where the road forks. Follow the road to the left and proceed along the track. Now you are walking out onto the heathland between White Meldon (right) and South Hill Head (left). At your back, behind Upper Kidston, is Hamilton Hill. Follow this track for about ¼ mile and you will come to a pathway on the left, this is your short detour to the Roman road. The path skirts South Hill Head, and meets the clearly defined Roman road at right angles.

This Roman road is all that is left of the old military way from

61

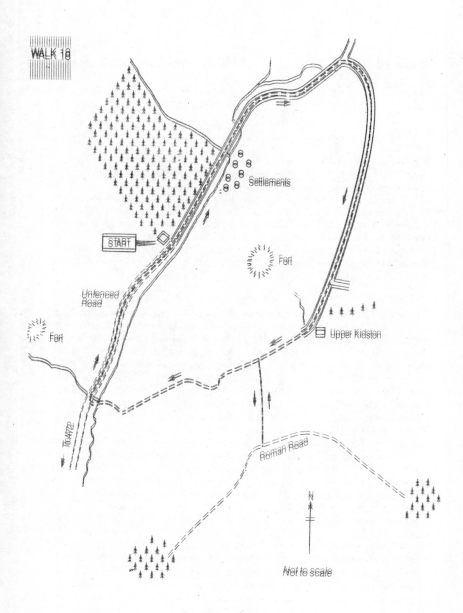

WALK 18

Settlements

Fort

START

Unfenced Road

Fort

Upper Kidston

To A702

Roman Road

N

Not to scale

Newstead (*Trimontium*: See Walk 30) to Lyne, now a neighbouring village to Peebles. Lyne was the site of an important Roman fort on the westward link road to the west coast route into Scotland (Carlisle to the *Vallum Antonini*=Antonine Wall). Today the line begins just a few yards out of Jedderfield plantation (low, to your left) and disappears (right) at Edston Hill plantation. The road follows the contours of the southern foothills of South Hill Head.

Walk back round the hill to the track and continue left. The way climbs then falls giving you good views of the Meldon Burn valley. The colour patterns of the valley floor are various tints of green, merging with the browns of the bracken and the darker, harsher shades of the heather. As you walk over the higher contours the eye catches curious mounds and bumps, probably the last resting place of some Iron Age headman.

For those interested in ornithology, this Border moorland offers a feast. Only the hardiest birds can survive the harsh winters up here, and the red grouse of the area, which feed on heather, have adapted stamina to fight back, and tread for long periods to avoid being buried in the drifting snow. By and large the birds here, of note, are usually scavengers or predators. Look for the predatory trio, the peregrine, the kestrel and the merlin, and listen for the food-searching scuffling of the black and red grouse, and the cries of the curlew, the plover and the greenshank.

Follow the track down the hill from South Hill Head towards Meldon Burn. Cross the burn and reach the unfenced macadam road, which marks the last lap of the walk. On the left is the village of Lyne, with the ivy covered Tower of Barns, the residence, in the sixteenth century, of William Burnet, a famous 'marauder', and one of the smallest churches in Scotland. This road takes you directly back to the beginning of the walk.

Special Interest: Palisaded settlements

The countryside abounds with remains of Iron Age Celts, in the south-east Borders. The earliest Celts hereabouts were known for the settlements they built of one or two huts enclosed by a palisade. Dates obtained by the radiocarbon method suggest their first occupation was in the sixth and seventh centuries. Up to 300 posts, cut from local timber, were needed to palisade the remains of the settlements you see on this walk.

The people who lived here were mostly of the tribe known as the Selgovae, and maybe those who had intermarried with their eastern neighbours, the Votadini. The dwellers in the palisaded settlements were a warrior-based society producing weapons and implements of iron, with a few gold ornaments to wear.

$4\frac{1}{4}$ miles (7 km)

OS sheet 73

Once the central part of the south-east Borders was a busy highway for the drovers, the men and their families who drove cattle, and later sheep, from Scotland to England, or from the Highlands to the markets of central and southern Scotland. The drovers were a hardy lot whose cattle trade was an established and important part of the Scots economy. The Scottish droving trade began in the lawless Highlands of the late sixteenth century and reached its peak in the nineteenth century. The decline in droving came when it was no longer necessary, or economic, to drive cattle many miles to market, and when sheep reigned supreme over cattle.

As the movement of cattle across toll roads, and across the Scottish–English border, was subject to tax, the drovers penetrated the Borderland with many 'secret' routes to dodge the tax. Avoiding regular routes, the drivers made their own rough roads many of which are traceable today. Those who would like to learn more of the background and life of the Scottish drovers are recommended to seek out Dr A.R.B. Haldane's definitive work on the subject, namely *The Drove Roads of Scotland* (new edition, David & Charles, 1973).

This walk begins at the youth hostel at Broadmeadows on the A708 north of Selkirk; it is well signposted. On your way from Selkirk, once you are past Harewood Glen, look for the signs for the birthplace of Mungo Park (1771–1806, famous Scottish traveller in Africa) and Foulshiels Farm, both on the right. Broadmeadows is about $\frac{3}{4}$ mile past Foulshiels as the road snakes over the two Yarrow bridges at Black Andrew Wood. Cross the second bridge and so into Broadmeadows, pass the hotel and follow the road round to the youth hostel.

Park, considerately, anywhere in the area. Take the footpath from the youth hostel north through the plantation, along the left-hand side of the burn. Walk to the end of the plantation and turn right along the path across the burn. A few yards from the burn the path meets another, which has come up from the A708, skirting Broadmeadows. Turn left onto the second path and continue on this path, where you will cross the burn twice more at two crossings close to each other. Following the path for about $\frac{3}{4}$ mile you will ascend to a great concourse of four tracks; north is the path to Yair Hill Forest, but across

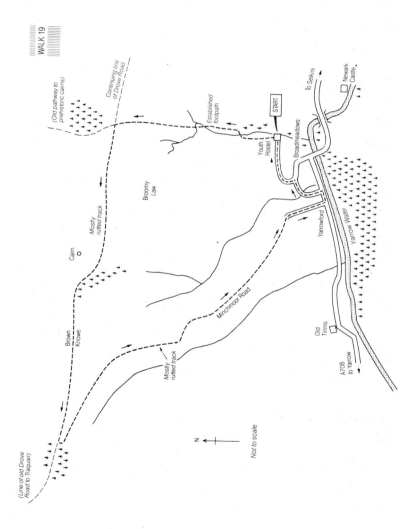

(Old pathway to prehistoric cairns)

Continuing line of Drove Road

Established footpath

START

Youth Hostel

Broadmeadows

To Selkirk

Newark Castle

Broomy Law

Mostly rutted track

Cairn

Yarrowford

Yarrow Water

Minchmoor Road

Brown Knowe

Old Tinnis

A708 to Yarrow

Mostly rutted track

(Line of old Drove Road to Traquair)

N

Not to scale

from right to left is the fine Traquair to Selkirk Drove Road. On your left is Broomy Law Hill.

Turn left onto the drove road and follow it as it skirts Broomy Law's footbridge and on your right you will see the twin cairns of Yair. Walk forward towards the plantation, which will skirt to the left until you meet an old path coming from the left at the edge of the plantation. In front of you is the Brown Knowe elevation of the Old Drove Road.

From the edge of the plantation it is 1 mile to the summit of Browne Knowe Hill. Pause here for a breather and contemplate the fine view. To your right and front, as you ascend Brown Knowe, is the great Elibank and Traquair Forest; to your left is the valley of the Hanging-shaw Burn down which you are to pass. This is a nice place to recall what Sir Walter Scott wrote in his story *The Two Drovers*, about the very men who trod this old road 'The Highlanders in particular are masters of this difficult trade of droving, which seems to suit them as well as the trade of war. It affords exercise for all their habits of patient endurance and active exertion. They are required to know perfectly the drove roads which lie over the wildest tracts of the country, and to avoid as much as possible the highway that distress the feet of the bullock, and the turnpikes which annoy the spirit of the drover; whereas on the broad green or grey track, which leads across the pathless moor, the herd not only move at ease and without taxation, but, if they mind their business, may pick up a mouthful of food by the way.'

This track has not changed much since the drover's day except that there are more trees to the west. Follow the drove road down past the cairn, on the right, to the edge of the wood. Here, it joins with another old road called Minchmoor Road. Turn left down the moorland track towards Yarrowford, between Whitehope Rig and Wanders Knowe.

About 1½ miles down Minchmoor Road, the track widens to two distinct marking boundaries, follow these, skirting Hangingshaw Plantation, to Yarrowford and its junction with the A708. Turn left at the main road, walk on for a few yards and then turn first left into the road leading to Broadmeadows and the youth hostel at the start of the walk.

Special Interest: Minchmoor Road

Minchmoor Road has seen some history. Down this track came the defeated army of James Graham, Marquis of Montrose, in September 1645 after the Battle of Philiphaugh. Sir Walter Scott immortalized the road when he made it the one down which the drovers, Robin Oig and Harry Wakefield, tramped in *The Two Drovers*. The road has been popular for walkers since the days it first appeared in William Thompson's maps of Peeblesshire (1821) and Selkirkshire (1824).

On a misty day at eventide as you walk you can imagine hearing the low of driven cattle and see the wraiths of the long-dead drovers fading into the haze; men given flesh and blood by such as J. Macky in *Journey through Scotland* (1723). 'They [the drovers] are mighty civil, dressed in their stached waistcoats, a trousing [which is breeches and stocking of one piece of striped stuff] with a plaid for a cloak and a blue bonnet. They have a poinard, knife and fork in one sheath hanging at one side of their belt, their pistol at the other and their snuff mull before with a great broadsword at their side. Their attendance [ie people with them] was very numerous all in belted plaids, girt like women's petticoats down to the knee; their thighs and half of the leg all bare. They had also each a broadsword and poinard.'

Walk 20   Glentress Forest

1–4 miles (1.5–7 km)

OS sheet 73

There are more than a dozen interesting walks in Glentress Forest, but the four commented upon here, are worthy of note. These walks are well established and are marked out by coloured waymarking posts. The posts are green and have coloured rings around the heads. A post with two or more coloured rings shows that the path is common to two or more walks. The walks, of course, can be covered singly or joined together, say two or three as one walk.

Glentress belongs to the Forestry Commission of Scotland, who welcome careful visitors. It must be stressed that, as on any walk, the walker enters the forest and uses the facilities entirely at his or her own risk. The forest comprises of eight large and twenty smaller blocks of woodland within a 6-mile radius of Peebles, and totals some 10,000 acres. The part of the forest through which these walks pass was purchased from the Haystoun Estate in 1920, thus becoming one of the first Forestry Commission areas in the south of Scotland. Most of the forest tracks were laid out in the 1930s.

Make your base, and safe parking, at Glentress Forest Office, which is located just north of Glentress village, less than 3 miles along the A72 from Peebles. The route from the A72 to the car park by the Forest Office is clearly signposted at the roadside.

Yellow walk   This walk of some 1,700yds can be easily done within the hour. It is a good walk for introducing children to forest walking and as a fine sample of what is to be found in the rest of the forest. The yellow markings form a loop.

Orange walk   This walk is some 2½ miles long. Begin at the yellow markers, turning right at the picnic area and follow the track until the yellow markers merge with the orange. Walk forward, Kirn Law will rise away to your right, until the orange markers merge with the blue at a fork. Turn left and follow the orange/blue markers for a few hundred yards. The orange markers will then meet the blue and red where you branch left round Cardie Hill, with its prehistoric hill-fort. The path skirts the flanking ramparts of the fort which is well worth an exploration. Follow the orange markers back to the picnic area via Falla Brae. There is only one section of this walk which is steepish.

Blue walk   Reach the starting point of this walk by following the yellow and orange markers away from the picnic site. Where the

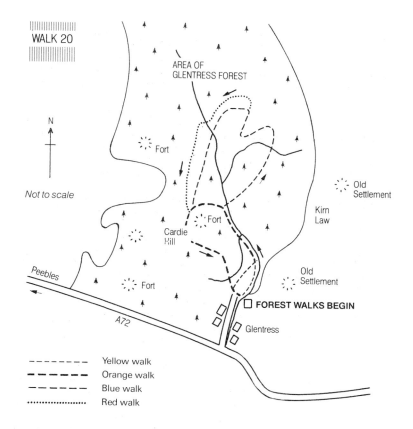

AREA OF
GLENTRESS FOREST

N

Not to scale

Fort

Old
Settlement

Kirn
Law

Fort

Cardie
Hill

Fort

Old
Settlement

Peebles

Fort

A72

□ FOREST WALKS BEGIN

Glentress

– – – – – – –   Yellow walk
▬ ▬ ▬ ▬ ▬ ▬   Orange walk
– – – – – –   Blue walk
··················   Red walk

orange and blue markers meet, leave the woodland track and follow the path right. After a few yards you will get onto a track again, follow this to a mid-forest picnic area. Once through this area, walk on down the track and follow the markers sharp left. Half a mile or so onwards, the blue markers merge with the red, so turn left here, leaving the forest track for a few yards across a woodland path. Where the path meets another woodland track it veers left, crossing a burn. Keep the burn now on your left and follow the markers to the concourse of red/blue/orange markers. Now you have a choice of following the orange markers left to the fort and Cardie Hill, or the less steep orange-yellow trail back. The blue walk itself is around 4 miles long.

This walk is a good one if you would like to study the management of trees. Even though most of the plantations walked through are coniferous—the sites do not have good enough ground for hardwood timber production for commercial use—there is a very large variety. Look for the Scots pine, the European and Japanese larch, the

Douglas fir, the Norway spruce, the Sitka spruce, and the few attractive silver firs. Remember that pines and larches have needles that stand free from the twigs and that pines have groups of up to five needles, while those of larches grow in clusters. Spruces are on woody 'pegs'. Silver firs have blunt buds, while Douglas firs have pointed buds.

Red walk   This is best reached by following the markers yellow to orange, to blue. This walk is almost $4\frac{1}{2}$ miles in itself and is at the heart of Glentress forest. It is a good afternoon's wander and is composed mainly of forest roads. Although it climbs higher than the other walks, in the lower slopes of Caresman and Kittlegairy hills, it is uncomplicated.

Above all the others the walk is good for observing the local wildlife, including wild flowers and plants. Have a close look at the burns hereabouts, despite their size they are used for spawning salmon and sea trout from the River Tweed. Keep a watch out for the roe deer of the forest. Fundamentally they are shy creatures and are most likely to be seen at dawn or dusk. As a rule they strip the bark off the trees as a mark of their territory and generally browse amongst the newly planted trees. Roe deer grow to only 2ft tall.

Glentress is ideal for a forest walk with a difference. Instead of following a marked route you can choose your own route by finding your way to various highlight points. The area of Glentress Forest has no less than six old settlements and forts to locate and explore. The Forest Centre at the car park will supply you with a map of control points. Each control point has a distinctive red and white wayfaring symbol on a post to aid identification. The nice thing about independent wayfaring is that you can make your walk as easy or as difficult as you wish. You can remain on forest paths for most of your walk, or head away from paths through the woodlands. This wayfaring course can also be used as a more serious orienteering venture by using a compass or a stopwatch for the walks.

4¼ miles (7 km)

OS sheet 73

An old royal burgh, Peebles has been famous for its woollen mills for decades. Once the area was popular with the royal Scottish court for its castle (now vanished), which was a note-worthy hunting lodge. Though less harassed than other towns near the border, Peebles was burned by the English more than once, and was occupied by Cromwell in 1649 and Bonnie Prince Charlie's forces in 1745.

The town still exhibits something of its medieval air, particularly in its Beltane Festival at the beginning of May. Originally this was a pagan thanksgiving to the god Baal for 'fire' (ie, the warm days in early summer) and attracted many famous people like James I and VI. Today Beltane Week is a great occasion in the town. It includes Riding the Marches, when horsemen ride around the town's boundaries, and the crowning of a Beltane Queen.

Begin the walk at the car park to the south of Tweed Bridge; the entrance to the car park is on the B7062 road to Innerleithen. From the car park face the river; cross the embankment by the steps and walk down to the river. Turn left and follow the riverside path until you come to the Tweed Bridge (begun in 1467 and widened in 1834 and 1900). Follow the path up the side of the bridge and onto the road. Cross the road and descend to the riverside walk by way of the steps. Soon you will come to a weir—a nice place to stop and contemplate the river. Here in September, October and November you can watch the great activity of the salmon anglers. This stretch of the Tweed is known as the Town Water and opposite the weir is the inflow of the Eddleston Water, a popular spot for eel fishing. Past the weir (known locally as 'The Cauld') a bank of trees springs up on the left. Walk along until you come to a footbridge on the right, continue past an iron fence and walk round the Artist's Rock, a fine viewpoint.

Retrace your steps to just before the footbridge and bear right onto the grassy path. Cross the old railway line, walk through the gateway and across the field to the road. Turn right at the road, which, after a few yards, becomes a farm track. Walk on and turn left then right. Go over the stile and follow the path across fields to the crest of a rise, then follow the edge of South Park Wood. South Park Wood contains mature oak (both pedunculate and evergreen), elm (mostly wych),

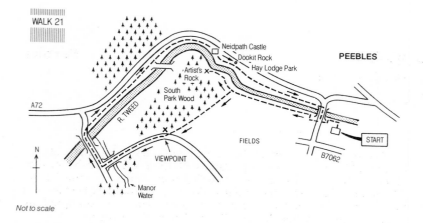

Neidpath Castle
Dookit Rock
Hay Lodge Park

PEEBLES

Artist's x
Rock

South
Park Wood

A72

R. TWEED

N

VIEWPOINT

Manor
Water

FIELDS

START

B7062

Not to scale

alder, silver birch, larch, Norway spruce, with a scattering of black and Lombardy poplars.

Wildlife is plentiful here, so look for the greater spotted woodpeckers, waxwings, swallows, martins, grey herons and the curious long-billed tree creeper. If you are lucky, too, you may catch a glimpse of roe deer, and red squirrels. The most common mammals around the edge of the wood are brown hares and rabbits.

Once past the wood you will come to a road. Turn right down the hill to a small bridge, on your right is the woodland of Manor Sware; also a popular viewpoint. Turn right at the bridge (called Old Manor Bridge) and walk down to the newer Manor Bridge spanning the Manor Water. Old Manor Bridge was built in 1703 to carry the Peebles road to Kirkton and was replaced in 1883 by Manor Bridge. Look out here for the wild mink!

Cross Manor Bridge and just beyond, turn right over a stile. Follow the riverside path for about 1 mile until you come to a railway viaduct. This seven-arched viaduct was opened in 1864 to take the Caledonian Line across the Tweed into Peebles; Note the tunnel cut into the hillside under South Park Wood. This line (alas little used) lost its passenger link in 1950 and was finally closed in 1962.

At the viaduct path, cross the stile and continue past Neidpath Castle into Hay Lodge Park. As you do so you will pass Dookit Rock. This rock takes its name from the old Scots word 'dooking', which means swimming. Here was an old diving board (you can still see the iron bolts on a rock at the edge of the river), a popular meeting place for Peebles folk in days of yore. Cross the plank bridge into Hay Lodge Park and meet up with the asphalt path. Continue along the riverside onto the Tweed Bridge, retrace your steps to the car park.

Special Interest: Neidpath Castle
This castle had its origins in the thirteenth century and was once a

stronghold of the Frasers. Later it became the home—originally it was a tower house—of the Earls of Tweeddale, whose crest (a goat's head) surmounts the gateway to the courtyard. The castle was extensively altered by Lord Yester, who rebuilt the present gateway and extended the terrace gardens, traces of which can still be seen. A supporter of Charles II, Lord Yester (he was also second Earl of Tweeddale) unsuccessfully tried to hold the castle against Oliver Cromwell. The castle was purchased in 1618 by the 1st Duke of Queensbury. The 4th Duke, known to all as the profligate 'Old Q', despoiled the estate to spite his heir. When Wordsworth visited the area he wrote a sonnet beginning 'Degenerate Douglas! Oh the unworthy lord!' to mourn the wasting of the estate. Today the castle is owned by the Earl of Wemyss and March, who opens the doors to the public at set times.

Rising in the Pentland Hills, the Water of Leith flows for 23 miles and meets the Firth of Forth at Leith. Its source is among the heather-covered moorland and rough pastures above East Colzium and flows into Harperrig, one of the City of Edinburgh's compensation reservoirs. This waterway was once crystal clear, for an Act of Scottish Parliament, in 1617, decreed that the standard pint jug was to contain 'three pounds seven ounces troye of cleane ryand water from the Water of Leith'. The water has deteriorated since then as the villages grew along its banks and at one time it became no more than an open sewer. Since 1896 much has been done to clean the river which now boasts large stocks of trout.

This walk begins in the village of Balerno, which is the last village in the chain of villages which are linked by the river valley which skirts the northern slopes of the Pentland Hills. It nestles on the west bank of the Bavelaw Burn near its confluence with the Water of Leith. *Blaeu's Atlas* of 1654 calls this area 'bryney' (that is, 'well-sheltered place'), which was then solely a farming community.

The A70 cuts near to the northern edge of Balerno, so take this road from the west via Lanark, or follow it out of Edinburgh (north-east) via Juniper Green and Currie.

All the way this is a walk of easy paths and gradients, a wander for observation. Park in the vicinity of Balerno Bank Paper Mill (1805), or Byrnie Paper Mill (1799, later a sawmill), which are both near the bridge over the Water of Leith.

Walk down Harelaw Road towards its junction with the A70, over the Water of Leith bridge. Once over the bridge look right for the path down to the riverside. Straight in front of you across the river on the Bavelaw Burn is Malleny House and Garden owned by the National Trust for Scotland. The origin of the house can be traced back to 1478. Bear right along the path between the tree-clad banks. The ruin which appears now on your right across the water is that of Newmills Grain Mill, within the bounds of the Old Mill House, Newmills. The mill was destroyed by fire but the grindstones are still intact. Walk on down the path as it is squeezed near the A70 (known locally as Lanark Road) and then swerves away and narrows once again.

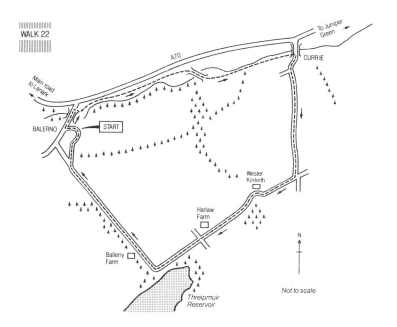

Where the Water of Leith widens to take in a small island, look high up in the wood for Lennox Tower. Little authentic history is known of the ruined building but plenty of legend is associated with it. Now the path veers away from the river for a few yards and you pass a group of interesting buildings. These edificies by the waterside, close to the bridge, are the site of Waulk Mill of Ballernoch, which was granted a charter in 1736 as a filling mill. It became a distillery in 1763, and around 1900 was known as Kinauld Farm (it is now a piggery).

Ignore the link footpaths leading up to Lanark Road and make for the bridge over to the other bank of the Water of Leith. By this time you will be well aware of the flora and fauna of the district. The Water of Leith valley provides the principal wildlife corridor between the uplands of the Pentland Hills and the urban area. This walk provides an excellent exercise in tree-spotting, as well as wild shrubs and other flowering plants. All around there are about 150 different plant species, as well as a variety of birds and much evidence of badgers and roe deer.

Just over the bridge, look back (left) over the water and see the former Balerno Papermill which was established in 1788. After 1882 it became a glue works and it is now a tannery. Not far along on the right, notice the stone retaining walls of the railway embankment. These have long been used for practice climbs by enthusiasts, including Dougal Haston, the famous mountaineer who lived in Currie as a

75

child. (Haston was killed in 1975 in Switzerland not long after his renowned Everest expedition.)

By now you will have realized that the footpath follows the line of the old railway, and you are now approaching platform one of Currie Station, which was once packed with walkers and pioneers in high summer. At the station, walk up onto the Balerno-Harelaw Road and turn right. The bridge to your left as you turn into the village is called Currie Brig and reputedly dates from 1378. The bridge unites the two parts of Currie village, which was a small community centred on town farms. The name Currie was probably from the Latin *coria*, a meeting place, or the Gaelic *curagh*, a mossy dell.

Before you stride away forward look around for a minute or two. Away to your right was located Currie Mill—the remains of the kiln can still be seen—established in 1506. Look left now and forward to Currie Kirk, between the old schoolhouse and the former school. This area has been a place of worship for over 1,000 years, for along the river is the Well of St Mungo (destroyed by the railway excavation).

Follow this road up towards the summits of Harbour Hill and Bell's Hill, and turn left at the crossroads. Walk on through the steadings of Wester Kinleith. The elevation here gives you a fine view of the valley of the Water of Leith and its four old villages of (from left to right) Balerno, Currie, Blinkbonny and Juniper Green. Follow the road straight over the little crossroads at Harlaw Farm. You are now passing the foothills of Blackhill, and on your left is Threipmuir Reservoir. Follow the road sharp right and down past Balleny Farm which leads to Malleny Mills. The road brings you safely and directly back to your parking area in Balerno.

Special Interest: Papermaking community
The natural springs of the Pentland Hills hereabouts encouraged the setting up of papermills during the period 1776 to 1792. These required large amounts of water for processing and washing the linen and cotton rags from which the paper was made. Soon the industry was flourishing and during the latter half of the eighteenth century new paper mills were established at Juniper Green, Currie and Balerno. There were once ten papermills on the Water of Leith. All around the walk there are relics of the papermakers' community, life and work.

Walk 23   Almondell

2¼ miles (3·5 km)

OS sheet 65

Here is a very pleasant stroll around Almondell and Calder Wood which is by no means for the dedicated walker, but for those who wish to savour the atmosphere, the wildlife and the scenery of an old Scottish dell. All of this walk is along well-surfaced and clearly-defined walkways, so no special footwear is needed. To arrive at the walk, take the A71 from Edinburgh, via Burnwynd and Linburn. As you pass the turning (left) for Mid Calder Station, look for the north lodge (right) of Almondell and Calder Wood parkland. Turn into the drive which will lead you to safe parking. The nearest built-up area reference is East Calder.

Walk from the car park towards the beginning of the Union Canal Feeder, which was built between 1818 and 1822, to divert water from the River Almond for the Union Canal. Built by Irish and Highland navvies, the Union Canal was closed in 1965. From the estate road, walk south-west towards the metal aqueduct, along the right-hand side of the canal feeder. In the water you can see the long, grass-like plants called pondweeds and around this area you will find many varieties of wild flowers, among which are common lady's mantle, lady's smock, meadow saxifrage, water avens, hairy woodrush, leopardsbore, ramson's garlic and woodruff. Water shrews also live hereabouts.

Soon you come to the hut of the Lothians River Purification Board Station. This has instruments to collect and record information regarding the rate of water flow. Cast a glance over the feeder to the calibrated scales measuring the height of the water. On your right is the meadowland. Little is known of the history of the aqueduct which carries the feeder across the river. Just before you pass over the end of the metal viaduct you enter the Beechwood—you can't miss the fine beech trees. By the way, halfway up the elm tree (behind the post), there is a curious example of natural branch fusion (ie, natural grafting). As you walk on you will see a mixture of elm, ash, hawthorn, beech, sycamore and rowan. If you are lucky you might see something of the roe deer, or the willow warblers and tree creepers which frequent the area.

Now turn right onto the railway viaduct, and halfway across pause

77

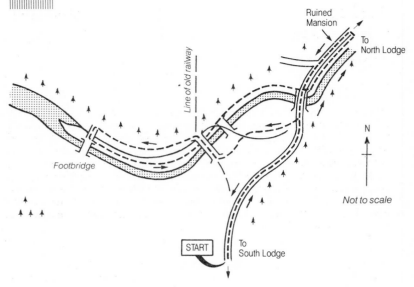

and look upstream and down. During the Carboniferous Period (ie 280 million years ago) Almondell was a large freshwater lagoon. See in the riverbed how the Ice Age exposed the Burdiehouse limestone. Just beyond the end of the railway viaduct are the shale dumps, relics of the oil shale extraction industry for between 1860 and 1960, oil, wax, tar and sulphate of ammonia were all extracted here. The viaduct was built to carry a mineral railway for the transportation of the shale. At the end of the viaduct turn left, pass through the trees and enter the grazed meadow strip along the hewn waterway. The trees here are mostly wych elms, with a few ash and tawny owls and kestrels may be seen. In summer a tube of insect repellent is useful against the midges and crane flies. Among the many clumps of nettles small tortoise-shell butterflies can be seen, the fallen trees hereabouts are good for fungus spotting and bush vetch and crosswort are among the wild flowers.

Continue along this stretch until you come to the footbridge. Turn left onto the first part of the footbridge then turn sharp left and follow the canal feeder's opposite stretch to the one down which you have walked. The footbridge leads to the new sewage works. On your right now is the River Almond, and across the river, the old sewage works, playground of hoards of scavenging black-headed gulls. The river islands here sport willows and alder, particularly mature examples of the white willow and of course plenty of rushes. The area abounds in wild flowers including monkey flower, Michaelmas daisy, red campion, tuberous comfrey, herb Robert and forget-me-nots. You may also see a weasel or two if you are lucky.

Walk on under the railway viaduct and up to the metal aqueduct, where you cross the feeder and arrive on the left bank of the River Almond. The sluice here is used by the Waterways Board. Across the river is a cliff of Burdiehouse limestone. You are now entering the sycamore woodland. As the path turns with the river the woodland is coniferous, with alder, Scots pine, spruce and larch. Cross the bridge and follow the path to Almondell Bridge (also called Nasmyth Bridge), cross the estate and get back to the water's edge. Descend to the riverside to a point below the waterfall. On the opposite bank is an anticline (80–100ft span), a tribute to the ingenuity of man. Take a moment to look back at the bridge, built by Alexander Nasmyth (1758–1840) to the order of Henry Erskine. Note the prominent rocks on the riverbed, these are sandstones.

Along the riverside you will see the stone which once was the sole bridge over the rivulet which comes down from Old Clapperton Hall. The stone was set up by Margaret Fraser, wife of David, eleventh Earl of Buchan, to Sir Simon Fraser, who was a keen supporter of Robert the Bruce. The stone reads: MARGARET COUNTESS OF BUCHAN DEDICATED THIS FOREST TO HER ANCESTOR SIR SIMON FRASER OCTOBER XV MDCCXXXIV. The yew tree over the stone dates from 1784. All around this part are what is known as ornamental woodland. Watch out for the pheasants. Keep children away from the (poisonous) shrub berries here in season. Trees to spot are lime, sweet chestnut, oak, copper beech, fir, cypress and sequoia. Follow the path through the lush waterside of London pride and periwinkle, water avens and yellow flag. If you are lucky you might see otters playing. Across the river is dedicated woodland. Note the 'erratic', boulders in a riverbed, sculpted by the glacial activity. Now walk on to the stables and walled garden (on the left), and a pebble beach at the end of the footpath. Turn up on to the estate road and turn left, this will bring you back to the car park (over Almondell Bridge). As you walk along the first section on the way back, you will pass the rear of the walled garden (remnants), the stables, a well, and the site of the old mansion house of the Earls of Buchan. Built by Henry Erskine, who died in 1817, it was lived in by the family until 1895. The house was blown up in 1969.

Walk 24
5 miles (8 km)

The Monk's Road

OS sheet 66

The Pentland Hills are a broken hill-range, stretching from 3 miles south-west of Edinburgh in a south-westerly direction for some 16 miles through the heart of Midlothian, Peeblesshire and Lanarkshire to near Carnwath. The northern tip of the Pentland Range lies within the boundary of the City of Edinburgh and runs along the summits of Caerketton and Allermuir (1,617ft). The Pentlands offer the walker a choice of delightful and not too arduous paths, many of them ancient 'Kirk roads', that is roads from hamlets to churches, and drove roads. The whole hill range is criss-crossed with paths, many marked by the guide posts of the Scottish Rights of Way Society (and in places by irksome fences). The highest point is Scald Law (1,898ft). The hills are generally rounded, affording good pasture for sheep as it is a land of streams and reservoirs. It is well to note that this walk can be a wet one. Stout shoes are a good thing to have in wet weather, and there is one stream to ford.

To arrive at the beginning of this route, take the A702 from Edinburgh. Look for the junction with the A766 (left) and about ½ mile further on look for the junction right for Nine Mile Burn. Park in the region of the inn.

By the inn the minor road turns sharp left (on the line of the Old Roman Road). Here, you will see the path climbing ahead to Cap Law. Turn onto this well-defined path and you will be walking in some very holy footsteps. This part of the walk was the old pilgrim route from the Cistercian monastery of nearby Newhall, over the Pentlands to Loganlee, and the ultimate goal of Holyrood Abbey (at the foot of Arthur's Seat, Edinburgh). All round this area are monastic relics; on your left is Monk's Burn and Spittal Hill—named after the outpost of Newhall monastery where wayfarers used to visit for supper and a night's accommodation.

Walk on between Green Law and Braid Law until you come to the stone to the right of the path. This is the base of an ancient cross, which marked the pilgrimage way. In 1835 some old copper coins were found in the socket of the stone. The path leads along and up to the lower contours of West Kip Hill. Here is a concourse of old paths. To the left is the old route to Bavelaw Castle, a seventeenth-century 'laird's house'. Turn right and skirt the wood at West Kip. The path is

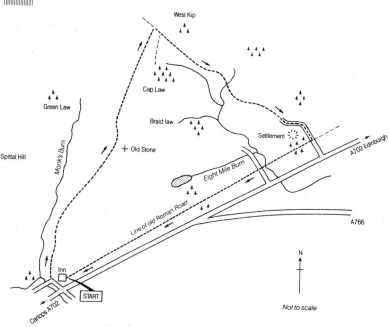

West Kip

Cap Law

Green Law

Braid law

Settlement

A702 Edinburgh

Spittal Hill

Monk's Burn

+ Old Stone

Eight Mile Burn

A766

Line of old Roman Road

N

Inn

START

Carlops A702

Not to scale

clearly defined and the views delightful. It's worth pausing to have a look at the geology of the Pentlands. The rocks of the Pentlands are carboniferous, that is, they date from the Palaezoic era, some 200 to 500 million years ago. Most of the volcanic rocks around this walk are composed of Silurian strata and worth looking at for fossils. During the Palaezoic period there appeared the first fish, amphibians and reptiles. The path descends to Eastside where it meets a minor road, fenced and unfenced in parts, which leads ultimately to the A702. As the road descends you can't miss the ancient prehistoric settlement on the right.

Just before the junction with the A702, the road on which you are now walking bisects the line of the old Roman Road to the west. (If you are interested there is another section of this Roman way just past Carlops on the A702 from Hartside to Stonypath.) Turn left onto a ditched road which will take you to Eight Mile Burn and a road to Quarrel Burn Reservoir. In wet weather this path can be somewhat squelchy. Cross Eight Mile Burn and the reservoir road and get onto the Roman Road again; it is almost straight, between two banks of trees and takes you directly back to the inn at Nine Mile Burn. The 'Eight Mile' and 'Nine Mile' references are to Roman miles where there would be rest posts during the Occupation.

Walk 25   East Cairn Hill

6 miles (9·5 km)

OS sheet 65

East Cairn Hill on the northern edge of the Pentland Hills, overlooks the broad central valley of Scotland. Below it runs the Cauldstane Slap, an ancient cattle-drovers' track which itself can be followed for 8 miles from West Linton golf course, by the A702, to the A70 beyond Harperrig reservoir. The walk rates high amongst the selection here in terms of scenery, but the conditions have to be right. The hilltops should be clear, but even so, photographers will find the panorama difficult to freeze on film for the vastness of nature refuses to be harnessed. At East Cairn Hill one has to be content with feasting the eye. The going is rough and one section of the walk is through springy, ankle-aching heather.

For the start of this walk take the A70 out of Edinburgh via Currie and Balerno. This is the main road, too, from Lanark.

The walk starts at the curiously named Little Vantage. Park at the old ruin on the left-hand side of the A70 out of Edinburgh. The ruin is of an old inn which was once a change-house (ie for changing teams of horses) in the old coaching days. Walk from the ruin, down the A70, to the old Drove Road, which forms the bulk of the walk. Take care, as this is a busy road in summer, and walk facing the traffic.

Turn left onto the drove road and walk forward. Walk on until the road has crossed four burns, and until the Baad Park Burn comes up on the right to run parallel with the road (which is well marked by footslog and posts). Pause here for your first long view.

On your right is Harperrig reservoir into which the Water of Leith discharges. At the far end of the reservoir are the ruins of East Cairns Castle, which once belonged to Sir George Crichton, High Admiral of Scotland. As a public-spirited action his men guarded this track you are on, through the Pentlands, in the days before it was a drove road, for it was a track for robbers and outlaws before the cattle drives. Flanking the castle is West Cairns Plantation.

Walk forward and up, keeping the plantation in sight on the right; when you draw level with the end of the plantation leave the drove road and walk (left) across the heather and make for the top of nearby East Cairn Hill. There are several sheep runs up to the top, so you can either choose one of these to ascend, or test whether or not you have

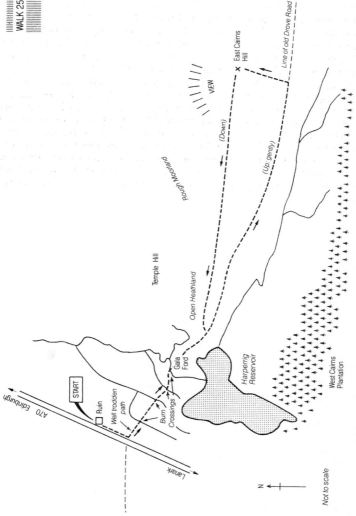

WALK 25

VIEW

East Cairns Hill x

Line of old Drove Road

(Down)

(Up: gently)

Rough Moorland

Temple Hill

Open Heathland

Gala Ford

Harperrig Reservoir

West Cairns Plantation

START

Ruin

Well trodden path

Burn Crossings

A70

Edinburgh

Lanark

N

Not to scale

weak ankles by springing through the heather. At the top of the hill is a cairn, and the breathtaking view of the environs of Edinburgh and more of Scotland than you could see in a week. On your far right is Threipmuir reservoir. The name comes from the old Scots word 'threep', to send your hunting dogs off in pursuit of game. The name dates from the time when Sir William St Clair of Roslin used to hunt wild deer here with Robert the Bruce. This long ridge between East Cairn Hill (where you are standing) and West Cairn Hill (to your left) is called Cauldstane Slap, the haunt of brigands; the place is mentioned by R.L. Stevenson in *Weir of Hermiston*.

If you are interested in ornithology, you will have noticed the Pentland birdlife already. In truth, the Pentlands do not show any remarkable features of birdlife which bring naturalists on special visits, but there is certainly a remarkable variety of species to be seen.

When you are ready to go on, face the A70 from the cairn and get your bearings. See how the drove road snakes to meet it. Cut down the heather in a straight line from the cairn, until you meet the drove road by the edge of Harperrig reservoir. The drove road brings you back to the A70, onto which you turn right (watch the traffic!) to return to the ruin.

Walk 26

Capelaw and Clubbiedean

6½ miles (10·5 km)

OS sheet 66

This walk starts at Bonaly Tower. Originally a farmhouse, it was altered in 1845 by Henry Thomas, Lord Cockburn (1779–1854), the famous advocate and author of the classic *Memorials of his Time* (pub. 1856). There was a village hereabouts from 1652, with a flourishing distillery, tannery and magnesia factory, but all have now disappeared, leaving the centrepiece of Bonaly Tower.

From Edinburgh (Princes Street West) take the A70 to its junction with the A720 at Juniper Green. Turn right along the A720 to Colinton, cross the river and take the first turning right, then the second right and follow the road to Bonaly Tower. Parking here needs some thought in high summer as it is a popular area, but there should be ample parking space on verges. You will need a sturdy pair of calves for this walk, and good walking shoes, for it's up hill and down dale.

Walk down the tree-lined road to the left past the tower and through the thicker belt of trees (you pass under the electricity lines on pylons). At the end of the macadam road you join the well-defined path for Capelaw Hill. There should be guide posts along the path, but they are fair game for vandals. Follow the path and it will bring you past Bonaly reservoir on your right. Cross the burn and you are now walking around the foot of Capelaw Hill. The way curves to the right then left. Walk on, over another burn, and where the path crosses the burn, you have traversed the district boundary and are now walking round the foot of Harbour Hill (right).

This path is taking you towards Glencorse reservoir, so pause a while and take in the view. The three hills in front are, left to right, Turnhouse Hill, Carnathy Hill and Scald Law (the highest of Pentlands). At the foot of Turnhouse Hill lies Glencorse reservoir, like a boomerang; beneath the waters are the ancient ruins of St Katherine's in the Hopes. The chapel existed as early as 1230 and was supported by the monks of Holyrood for Pentland travellers. 'Hopes' comes from the Scottish word 'hope', meaning a hollow among the hills. At the foot of Turnhouse Hill is a battlefield, where the covenanters confronted the parliamentarians under Dalziel of the Binns, which led to the defeat and flight of the covenanters in 1666.

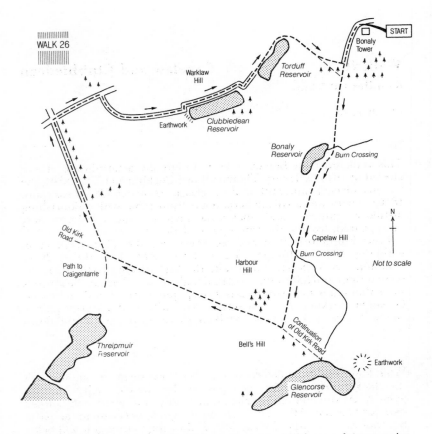

START
Bonaly
Tower

Torduff
Reservoir

Warklaw
Hill

Clubbiedean
Reservoir

Earthwork

Bonaly
Reservoir

Burn Crossing

N

Old Kirk
Road

Capelaw Hill

Burn Crossing

Not to scale

Path to
Craigentarrie

Harbour
Hill

Continuation
of Old Kirk
Road

Threipmuir
Reservoir

Bell's Hill

Earthwork

Glencorse
Reservoir

Away to the left of the reservoir is an Iron Age hill fort and souterrain. The whole presents an unfolding panorama of Penicuik and the far Moorfoot Hills. If you come to this place at dusk you may encounter a strange figure jogging down the path to Glencorse reservoir—a skeleton in running shorts. The local story tells of a schoolteacher from Balerno who, in 1908, was drowned in Glencorse reservoir while out running.

The path from Bonaly reservoir leads close to a belt of trees at the shore of Glencorse reservoir, here it meets the old 'Kirk road' (which is just a path) from Currie. Turn right onto this path and walk up the gulley—past the thick belt of trees on the right—between the two hills of Bell's and Harbour. As you leave the gulley you cross the district boundary again.

On your far left is Threipmuir reservoir, and halfway down this stretch of the path, are branches to the left to the reservoir; ignore this and walk straight on to a crossing of the way lower down the hill. Turn right and follow the path down to the macadam road by the long phalanx of trees.

Walk down the road, which is at first partially fenced and then completely fenced, to the crossroads. Turn right for Middle Kinleith, ignoring the first turning right, and walk on to where the road forks. Straight on is Easter Kinleith and Warklaw Hill. Turn right and follow the road round to Clubbiedean reservoir. Keep following the road round the shore of the reservoir (noting the earthwork at the far side of the water), cross the bridge and you come to Torduff reservoir. Look up the hill to the left and you will see the outcrops of Torphin and the links.

At the end of the reservoir turn right and you will come to a path which forks after a while. Make your choice, as both take you back to the beginning of the walk.

Beecraigs Wood, which has been set out in recent years as a country park, is situated in the uplands of Bathgate Hills, some 2 miles south of Linlithgow. The walk is one of woodlands, grasslands, a loch and burns, all providing a habitat supporting a profusion of wildlife. Few people who speed down the nearby M9, between Edinburgh and Glasgow, or are making for the Highlands, realize that this delightful walk exists.

To get to it, take the Preston House road from the A803 from Linlithgow, go under the railway bridge and make for Beecraigs Wood. Once at the wood ignore the sweep of the road to the right and enter the wood. Soon you will come to the car park and picnic area, laid out in the wood by West Lothian District Council.

The walk begins in the car park. Cross the road into the wood straight ahead (it is marked). Walk all the way through the wood to the road. These woodlands of spruce, pine and larch give plenty of natural cover for roe deer—a timid deer, only 2ft tall, which hides by day in the open woods; and badgers, whose lives centre on the sett, a network of underground tunnels and who are usually nocturnal. Strangely enough, in the wood these larger mammals are the most frequently seen of the woodland creatures. Here too are rabbits, hares (the brown variety), weasels (Britain's smallest flesh-eating mammal) and stoats, who live in dens, and whose coats change from brown to white in winter. Seventy species of birds have been recorded in the area.

Once on the road turn right and walk towards the Linlithgow direction for a few yards. Look left for the woodland path up to Cockleroy fort. From here can be seen (left), Lochcote reservoir and the remains of Craigend castle, the fort at East Carribber, and (right) the waterfronts of Bo' ness and Grangemouth.

Follow the fort path back to the road and turn right. Walk down the road, past the path on which you first come out of Beecraigs Wood and look for another path on your left (opposite to the minor road to Kipps). Turn into this woodland path and walk along it until you reach a sharp bend right. From the bend cut left through the wood to your first path and follow it back to the car park. Pass the car park and

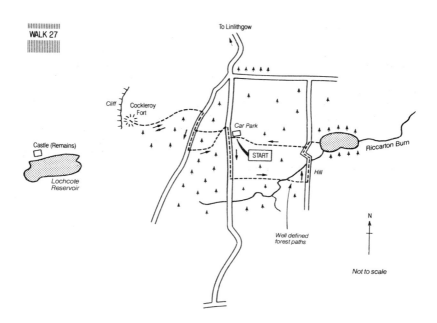

To Linlithgow

Cliff
Cockleroy Fort

Castle (Remains)

Car Park

START

Riccarton Burn

Hill

Lochcote Reservoir

Well defined forest paths

N

Not to scale

take the woodland path marked loch. This will bring you to the main road, cross this and take the path to the loch.

Up to 500 ducks winter on this 20-acre loch. The shelter, protection and food provided by the loch and its surrounding woodlands are a sanctuary for mallard (the male is the decorative one), pochard, widgeon, teal and golden eye. The flowers to note near the loch and throughout the woodland are butterfly/marsh orchids, foxgloves, stitchwort, vetches and bedstraw. By this time, of course, you will have realized that the walk is good for orienteering.

When you have had your fill of the lochside, come back onto the road and turn left. Walk along the road and past the left turn to Beecraig, on your left, too, are Riccarton Hills and Longmuir Plantation. Climb the hill to another track. Turn right onto the track, which will bring you to the car park.

If you have been noticing the markers for 'trout farm' and 'deer farm', follow them, it's worth the effort. The trout farm is run on commercial and educational lines. Incidentally daily permits to fish for rainbow and brown trout are available on site. The deer farm is well stocked with red deer, comprising a 12-pointer stag and follower hinds and yearlings. There's a 'safe path' through the deer farm which provides close-ups of Scotland's indigenous red deer. NOTE: Dogs should be kept on a lead when visiting the deer farm.

Special Interest: Cockleroy

The denuded remains of an Iron Age fort, sometimes known as Cuck-le-Roi, or Cocklerue, stands at the 912ft summit. The line of the main wall can be seen as well as an additional wall on the north-west; a superb situation. It has been a magic place for centuries. First were the Druids, that caste of priests among the Celts who enacted rituals here. They are credited with sorcery and witchcraft, and with the power of changing the weather. Druidic enchantment was deemed to cause death. In Elizabethan times, people came here with 'drummes abeating and folke adancing' to greet the morn of Mayday, and gather dew on the summit for 'magicke' purposes—least of all, the smear on the face to become beautiful.

5½ miles (9 km)

OS sheet 80

If you are a sucker for moors, Roman remains and hill flora, then this is the walk for you. The moorland flowers that you are most likely to see on this walk include sheep's sorrel, sow-wort, bog pimpernel, crowberry, cranberry, bog myrtle, butterwort, tormentil, bog asphodel and sundew. It is a walk for summer or very good weather, for although the walk itself is not forbidding, the elements make it so. Wind and driving rain can make the walk difficult and snow and fog render it almost impossible. Snow lies long in the Vales of Hindhope and Scotland's share of Upper Coquetdale. It is a walk over wild moorland flanked by the forests of Leithope and Redesdale, and the Hindhope Burn and the Grindstone Burn. Part of the walk is the Coquet Head stretch of the Pennine Way to the Roman Camps at Chew Green (Walk 30). You are in the heart, too, of the Cheviot Hills.

The walk starts from where the road from Hownam crosses the Hindhope Burn at Nether Hindhope. You arrive at Nether Hindhope by, either taking the A68 (T) Carter Bar to Jedburgh route, turning off at Edgerton via Pennymuir or by taking the B6401 from Yetholm via Hownam.

Park thoughtfully on the verge if the earth-surface lay-by is full. With your back to the way you arrived, turn down the minor road left, and almost immediately on your right is the footpath to take you up Hindhope Law. Go through the gate and over the burn. Walk up the moorland track towards the coppice of Corse Stack. It is a rising gradient of earth track and rubble. When you reach the summit of the track, Hindhope Law is on your left and Whiteside Hill is straight in front. Here is your first view of England and the long stretch of the Cheviot Hills all along the horizon. On your left are the slopes leading to Grindstone Burn. The Border is at the far line of trees (Redesdale Forest).

Go on towards Whiteside Hill; the track takes you upwards to the summit and now runs parallel to a burn, a tributary of the Hindhope Burn. Here, the old folk say, you can see shades of the Roman cavalry disappearing into the mists on certain days! A few yards after the burn peters out, the track makes a K-junction with your route back and the Pennine Way, now on its last leg to Yetholm. Turn off onto

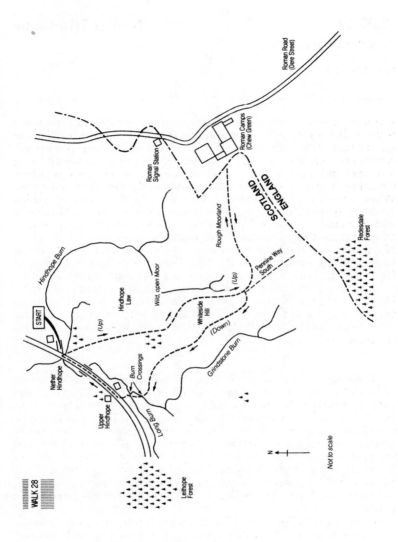

Roman Road
(Dere Street)

Roman Camps
(Chew Green)

ENGLAND

SCOTLAND

Roman
Signal Station

Redesdale
Forest

Rough Moorland

Pennine Way
South

Hindhope Burn

Wild, open Moor

(Up)

Hindhope
Law

Whiteside
Hill

(Down)

START

(Up)

Burn
Crossings

Grindstone Burn

Nether
Hindhope

Long Burn

Upper
Hindhope

N

Not to scale

Leithope
Forest

WALK 28

92

the clearly marked Pennine Way, east. You are now crossing Coquet Head and are heading towards Brownhart Law (far left). Walk on until you come to the Border between Scotland and England and, if you wish, walk further on and have a look at the Roman camps at Chew Green.

Had you been here in AD 211, when Britain was divided into two provinces of Roman Britannia, and when York (*Eburacum*) became capital of the Northern Province, you would already have been spotted by the Roman *classicum signum* (military signalers) at Brownhart Law signal station. You would have seen the sentries yourself as you stood on Coquet Head, at Chew Green Camp. Here there is a good deal to investigate. There was a marching camp here from the first century, which developed into a series of camps forming a Fortlet. The main camp had a 10ft ditch and there is evidence of streets and storage pits, indicating prolonged occupation of the area. If you look closely you can seen the lines of the ramparts and ditches of the camp annexes, which were probably used as waggon parks or shelters for military convoys on the way to *Trimontium* (Newstead) via Dere Street (Walk 30). A chapel was built within the confines of the fortlet, and at a later stage, in the days of the drovers, there was a wayside inn. This walk has undoubtedly seen the comings and goings of history.

Retrace your steps back along the Pennine Way to the K-junction again. Then turn left along the path across the summit of Whiteside Hill (the track along which you came to this place is now snaking down to your right). The walk is now downhill on rough track. You are soon walking midway between the far coppices of Corse Stack and Park Law and there are good views of the valleys of Leithope Forest (far left) all around. Grindstone Burn is on your left, and the track winds nearer to it all the time. At length the track meets the burn, cross it and follow the track sharp right. Cross the Long Burn, which meets the Grindstone Burn here and get onto the minor road. Follow the minor road through Upper Hindhope and over the bridge to where you parked.

Walk 29   Heatherhope

6½ miles (10·5 km)

OS sheet 80

Heatherhope Water is the least visited of the Cheviot 'lakes', yet it is full of character and its views are superb. The haunt of a wide variety of hill flora and fauna, it is the centre of a prehistoric settlement area and shows off the ruggedness of Cheviot outcrops and screes. Part of the walk is an old drove road and, save for the few conifers near the beginning of the walk, it is treeless, but by no means nude landscape. Tradition has it that heather will not grow on the land close to the Scotland/England border because of some deficiency in the soil. The hills around Heatherhope Loch prove that this is an old wives' tale.

This is the rolling yellow grassland of the Cheviot Hills, with the Cheviot, at 2,574ft, the summit of the range. It is a spacious land of limitless horizons, whose romantic and violently bloody past inspired Sir Walter Scott to write *Redgauntlet* and Rudyard Kipling to write *Puck of Pook's Hill*. On these hills fleet golden plover, redshanks and wheatear, while around the water, goldcrest and the smaller fellows of British ornithology can be seen.

To reach this walk make for Hownam (old spelling Hounam), which lies south-east of Morebattle (2 miles from Town Yetholm on the B6401). Park at Greenhill which is due south-east of Hownam; the walk is directly round the hills of the loch. The walk is by no means a marathon, but stout shoes or walking boots are a must. Distance here is not so much the tone as terrain and rubbly gradients. It's a walk for a nice day, with a picnic as an interlude.

The walk starts at the fork of the road at Greenhill, where it goes on south to The Yett. Between leaving the car and the footpath—which forms two-thirds of the walk—is a short stretch down the valley of the Heatherhope Burn. Where the minor road crosses the burn, a footpath goes off left. This is a public access area and is the best way round to walk. Climb up this path following, for three-quarters of the way, a tumbling tributary of the main burn. The path upwards is well defined. Keep on going until you leave the tributary down on your right and make for the crossed paths. Here your footpath, called The Kip path, or the path to Hownam Rings (a prehistoric settlement) now meets the last long arm of the drove road known as The Street on its way to England.

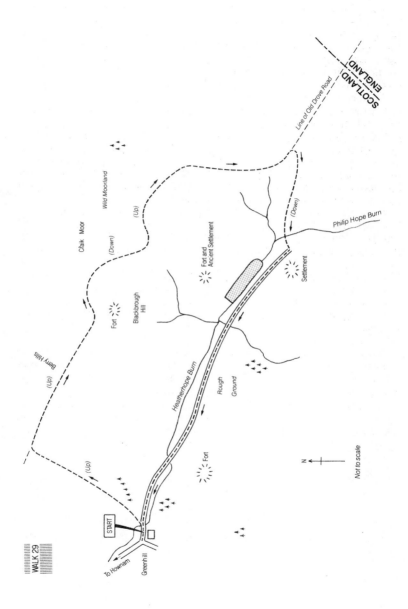

WALK 29

START

To Hownam

Greenhill

Heatherhope Burn

Fort

Rough
Ground

(Up)

Berry Hills

(Up)

Craik   Moor

Wild Moorland

(Down)

(Up)

Fort

Blackbrough
Hill

Fort and
Ancient Settlement

Settlement

Philip Hope Burn

(Down)

Line of Old Drove Road

SCOTLAND
ENGLAND

N

Not to scale

Pause here and just soak up the view. Far away in front of you—as you face Heatherhope Loch below—is the Border Line and Northumberland, a view which is with you until you turn at the foot of Belshaws Knowe. To your right, and from right to left, is Henshaw Law, Green Hill, Church Hope Hill, Dun Rig and Mozie Law. This is the kind of view written about in epics and which inspires concertos. Immediately below is Blackbrough Hill and beyond the prehistoric fort and settlement facing Mid Hill.

Turn right at the crossway and walk forward. After a few yards the old drove road forks; take the right-hand fork as the way is better. (The left-hand fork brings you back to the same drove track, further along.) Follow the drove road—note the hill-forts on your right and the typical Cheviot screes—as far as you can see. Your way is upwards and you pass through, in turn, Berry Hills, Craik Moor and the step plateau between Mow Law and Mid Hill. Just after Craik Moor you begin to drop down into the valley of Singingside Burn and rise again past the old settlement above Calroust Burn.

Keep on climbing out of Singingburn valley and you will join a footpath from the right. By now, of course, you have passed Mid Hill and Heatherhope Loch in the valley. Take this path that met you from the right, it keeps climbing to the walk's highest point—above Philip Hope Burn. On the crest have another inspirational observation. Your back is now to the Border Line. Below you is Heatherhope Loch. The highest hill, on the left of your vantage-point is Beefstand Hill, over whose crest passes the Border Line. From here a necklace of forts, cairns and settlements stretches back to Greenhill. From here too you can see The Street winding its way past Mozie Law and round to Black Braes, just into England.

Now, and for the rest of the walk, the going is easy. Down you go to Heatherhope Loch. You meet the beginning of the loch's minor road where the track crosses the Philip Hope Burn coming in from the left. Just up from this junction is the old prehistoric settlement of Church Hope Hill. The minor road now takes you directly to where you parked at Greenhill, past Heatherhope Burn—note the fort and settlement up on the hills, and the screes and outcrops—and along the course of its main outlet, the Heatherhope Burn.

Walk 30   Roman Dere Street

OS sheets 66/73/80   Divided into sections to explore by car and on foot

---

Introduction

Roman roads have a fascination all of their own and are recognized by their directness from place to place. The Romans constructed more than 6,000 miles of roads in Britain, and provided for centuries of transport. Some Roman roads still remain main routes, others are secondary; some too are revealed as field tracks and others are parish boundaries. All together they make intriguing walks, whether tackled as short stretches, long marathons or as 'detective' projects tracing their length on foot.

The main Roman road through the area covered by this book is called Dere Street, the northern prime route of the Romans to Scotland. Its full length is from York to the Firth of Forth and the Antonine Wall. It is sometimes called (perhaps erroneously) the northern branch of Watling Street, and was built as a consequence of the Roman Consul of Britain, Gnaeus Julius Agricola's first Scottish Campaign of AD 79–81.

The Roman roadbuilders had a great many problems as they pushed forward the ditches, tracks and stone slabs which made up the causeway of Dere Street through the Borders. Trees had to be felled and undergrowth cleared. A wide clearing had to be made on each side of the road and embankments had to be constructed, and rivers either had to be forded or bridged in some way. Quite often the quarries and pits that provided the material for road building had to be discovered by the *finitores* (surveyors) and *pavimentarius* (paviours). The Roman army was responsible for the construction of Dere Street. Trained military surveyors mapped out the route by means of a *groma*. This was a staff, spiked for insertion in the earth, carrying a pivot with four equal arms, set at right angles in the fashion of a cross. These were made of wood and covered with metal. Each *groma* carried a *perpendiculum* (plummet) and plumbline. Alignments could thus be taken by a pair of plummets and a distant pole or signal fire. The sections of Dere Street would be direct between two points of alignment, being careful to avoid natural obstacles.

Statius, the Roman author, gave practical advice in AD 90, for the building of roads like Dere Street. Ditches on either side marked the limits of the road, and the soil was removed from between them in order to provide a solid base. The width between the ditches for major

97

stretches of road was 84ft, and the *agger* (embankment) was some 50ft. This was solidly built up of stone, using gravel, with stone curbs, and a good drainage was provided. On occasions timber from the Border forests might be used to make the foundation of Dere Street. The bed of the road could be cobbled in clay, or large stones. Rammed gravel built up the road, and thus could be several feet in thickness.

Dere Street carried couriers and officials as well as legions of soldiers. A certain amount of slow transport would appear on Dere Street, including ox-waggons. To assist travellers in finding their way, milestones were set up at distances of 1,000 Roman paces (1,620 yards); they were cylindrical in shape and carried inscriptions, and gave not only distances, but names of emperors. The volume of trade with Scotland, of course, was considerable. There were *mansiones* (hotels) at distances of about 25 miles on Dere Street, and relays of horses were provided. To travel 50 miles in a day was considered an average journey. More surveillance than usual would be given to the miles of Dere Street which passed through Scotland, for this was the land of the hostile tribesmen called the Selgovae and the Votadini, whose 'capital' is thought to be the great protected settlement on Eildon Hill North, near Melrose.

Dere Street is regarded as a national monument in Scotland, and small notices are placed on gates to indicate its direction, which in many places is difficult to determine. This difficulty has been furthered by the fact that the Roman surveyors did not *construct* the full length of Dere Street on its journey into Scotland—*Bremenium* (High Rochester) to *Trimontium* (Newstead), to Cramond, a total of 68½ miles. More than in any other country the surveyors were able to use established and ancient tracks.

Section A: 22 miles (35 km)   Chew Green to Newstead

Including walk: Pennymuir to Whitton Edge 7 miles (11 km)

The Roman camps at Chew Green, on Brownhart Law (1,550ft), form the great launching area to take Dere Street into Scotland. The name was first used as Deorestrete, from the Saxon *deor*, meaning 'wild', by Simeon of Durham in his *History of St Cuthbert*, 1104–1108. The Roman road crosses the modern border at Brownhart Law signal station. This is a rectangular dugout with rounded corners, measuring 54 × 41ft—the ramparts were 18ft thick, and the east entrance faces Dere Street and protects it for a few yards with ditches. Past Greystone Brae, the Roman road darts back into England, but enters Scotland again at Black Halls. Now it skirts Gaisty Law and makes for the cairns at Blackhall Hill. Along this section the road consists of a low mound expanding to 17ft wide. Quarries for road materials can be seen on each side and at times the road disappears below peat. Hereabouts the course is not straight, but it does make use of natural levels, such as the neck of land joining Blackhall and Hunthall hills. As it snakes its way to Tow Ford on the Kale Water, Dere Street passes Woden Law, once an important native fort or *oppidum*. This multivallate fort, 400 × 140ft shows signs of being a Roman army training area, and there are remnants of siege works. Rising to 1,388ft, the fort is a marvellous viewpoint for the line of Dere Street and the dozens of hill forts in the area. At Tow Ford, Dere Street crosses the Kale Water and passes by the several training camps of Pennymuir.

From Pennymuir to Whitton Edge is perhaps the best unspoilt stretch of Dere Street. It is a fine, but gradient-ridden, walk, much used as a farm track. Arrive here by turning off the A68 (Carter Bar to Jedburgh section) for Edgerston, via Edgerston Tofts and North Riccarton. Park carefully on the verge on the Middlesknowes to Pennymuir section.

Begin by having a look at the Roman camps at Pennymuir T-junction, which are the best-preserved Roman temporary camps in Scotland. (Figures refer to map.)

Camp 1   Set on a platform, encloses 42 acres and probably accommodated two legions; approx 1,705 × 1,080ft. Six gateways.

Camp 2   Lies within the south-east portion of camp 1; 960 × 410ft. Six gateways.

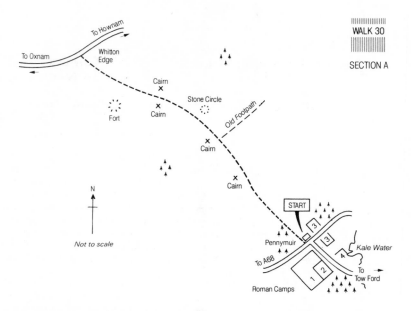

Camp 3   This camp is bisected by the modern Pennymuir to Hounam road; 910 × 640ft.

Camp 4   Camp on the other side of the Tow Ford road to camp 1; 350 × 150ft.

Start the walk at the ruin of Pennymuir Farm (on the main road by the plantation) where Dere Street bisects the modern road. All around the views are magnificent. The Roman road is clearly marked and the walk begins with a long straight stretch with a plantation to the left.

Dere Street proceeds across the fields to the north and passes a multitude of cairns and stone circles. The roadway cuts close first to Falla Knowe cairn, the next being Trestle Cairn just past the old footpath (going right) to Chatto Craig Fort and the prehistoric settlement of Swanlaws. Going on, and flanking Harkers Hill (left), is the most impressive Five Stones circle, closely flanked by Dere Street. Cunzierton Farm lies to the west and Cunzierton Hill was the site of a native fort. Some 15 miles to the north you can see the three hills of *Trimontium* (Eildons). This part of Dere Street is well worth walking in both directions, for the road section is interesting to study. The central mound of the road, about 22ft wide, can often be clearly detected and on either side the pits that were quarried for road material can be seen. In places the neglect of the old drainage system has caused swampy areas and elsewhere much has been lost by erosion, exposing the structure of the Roman road. This section climbs to a height of more than 1,000ft.

100

The last stretch of this walk along the Roman road is straight and rises directly to Whitton Edge, the road being limited on either side by field walls. The return starts at the Whitton road.

Dere Street turns sharp right at Whitton Edge. The section is partly covered by the present road, but there are deviations. Note the stone pits which were quarried for the Roman road, near Shotheids. The Roman surveyors took the road virtually straight over the Cessford Burn and it is now the shadow of the ruins of Cessford Castle (right), the grim fortress of the Kerr family. Passing south of Rennieston Farm, Dere Street is much overgrown on its sides and is a botanist's paradise. Through beech trees and varying scenery the road makes straight for Cappuck. Nowadays this is a single cottage, but in Roman times it was a Roman fortlet; the remains lie south of the cottage. The camp was constructed to guard the river crossing. The fort was approximately 290 × 218ft. At Cappuck an inscription was found which tells us about the soldiers who manned it and who constructed parts of the road. The stone reads: 'To Jupiter, Best and Greatest, a detachment of Roetians, spearmen in charge of Julius Severus, tribune, dedicated this . . .'

Dere Street now rises from Cappuck ford and proceeds as a double line of trees that leads to Crailinghall Bridge. North of the modern road is a well preserved section of the Roman road, 30ft wide. Now it crosses Ulston Moor where parts of it are worn to reveal the bottoming of large stones. Some of the later field walls are made of (vandalized) Roman road.

Beyond the bridge at Jerdonfield Park, on the river Jed, Dere Street is difficult to trace, but we do know the Romans forded both the Jed Water and the Teviot. It can, however, be seen near Woodside, north of Monteviot House where it continues at no great distance from the A68 north of Jedburgh. At Woodside the Roman road is easily detected to Lilliards Edge, to the left is the 1545 battlefield of Ancrum Moor, where the road is 22ft wide. Mirhouselaw, to the east, is a fine moated earthwork. Dere Street proceeds through the remains of Longnewton Forest to join the present road beyond Forest Lodge and thence to the disused railway line. The Roman road is now completely obliterated to Newtown St Boswells, but the line of it can be inferred on the lower eastern slopes of the Eildon Hills leading to Newstead.

Newstead is reached by following the A68 northwards and turning left at the B6361. The fort of Newstead was first built about AD 80 at the time of Agricola's great push into Scotland. Here, the timber framed buildings housed a crack cavalry regiment. For a detailed account of the excavations at Newstead see James Curle's book *A Roman Frontier Post and its People* (Maclehose, 1911).

Section B: 39 miles (62 km) Newstead to Cramond

Including walk: Kirktonhill to Soutra Aisle 5½ miles (9 km)
One division for walking, the rest by car

The fort of Newstead was to guard the crossing of the River Tweed. The site of the Roman bridge over the river was to the west of the fort and near to the present village. Just north of the Tweed the road is almost impossible to trace. A marching camp, discovered by aerial photograph, near Milsieburn Bridge indicates the direction of Dere Street.

Take the A7 (T) out of Melrose (to Galashiels), turn right where the road forks at Darnlee and go over the river following signs for Gattonside on the B6360. Roman Dere Street branched away to the left past Camp Knowe (by Gattonside Mains) through Faw Plantation, over Packman's Burn to Sorrowlessfield Mains and thence to Kedslie.

After looking at Camp Knowe, should you wish to do so, come back onto the B6360 and make for Leaderfoot. Turn left up onto the A68 (T) and follow this trunk road until you come to the turning (left) for Kedslie. Half a mile along this road you will come to a T-junction (road from Sorrowlessfield Mains). Here Dere Street joined an old track to Kedslie. This road, via Kedslie, Chapel Mains and Nether Blainslie is the modern line of Dere Street until it joins the A68 (T) again into Lauder. At St Leonard's (Hill) was a Roman camp of 165 acres with six gates. Pass through Lauder and make for Carfraemill. Look for the sign off left for Midburn and take it. Cross the line of the dismantled railway to the crossroads and turn right. This section of road through Oxton is the line of Dere Street. Go through Oxton and turn left for Mountmill. A few yards on, fork right onto the minor road for Kirktonhill.

Park safely at Kirktonhill and walk towards the markers for Roman camp and road. The modern settlement of Kirktonhill is right in the middle of a Roman camp. As the Roman occupation of Scotland was military, this permanent camp was for soldiers guarding the road, which passed right through it. The shape of the camp was rectangular with curved corners. Follow the road out of Kirktonhill onto the unfenced track, between the two flanking ditches of the camp. Where the track veers to the left, straight forward is Dere Street; the track has been in permanent use since the Romans made it.

This section of Dere Street is clearly marked. As you proceed, Turf

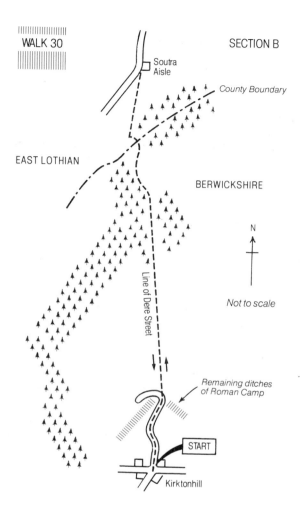

WALK 30

SECTION B

Soutra
Aisle

County Boundary

EAST LOTHIAN

BERWICKSHIRE

N

Line of Dere Street

Not to scale

Remaining ditches
of Roman Camp

START

Kirktonhill

Law is on your right. Follow the road into the plantation. It emerges again as the plantation appears again at the foot-ridges of Dun Law. The road across the moor widens to 27ft in parts. See how it is worn away in hollow ground, showing the extent of traffic over the ages. Where the line of Dere Street goes between the two arms of the plantation is the King's Inch, where lies the boundary of Berwickshire and East Lothian. Thence the Roman road bears round the trees to the B6368 at Soutra Aisle, the remains of a monastic chapel and pilgrim's refuge.

From Kirktonhill go back to the A68 (T) and drive north to Soutra Mains. Here, where the road crosses Dean Burn Bridge, the trunk road takes the line of Dere Street through Fala to Pathhead. Once through Pathhead, at Lothian Bridge the line of Dere Street turns left, over the ford towards Chesterhill. The long stretch of road from Chesterhill to Whitehill is the modern guise of Dere Street, to Dalkeith.

After Dalkeith the way of Dere Street is questionable—one course is a direct alignment on Castle Hill Edinburgh, to Cramond beyond. This was an important port and supply base for northern campaigns and the Antonine Wall. An alternative route would lie to Inveresk and the Firth of Forth.